ACHIEVING
YOUR
PINNACLE

A Career Guide for Actuaries

TOM MILLER

Lulu Publishing Services rev. date: 09/03/2013

Contents

5. The Interview Process

6. Tips for a Successful Actuarial Career

7. Appendix

Introduction

About the Author

Tom Miller is the managing partner of Pinnacle Group, one of the leading actuarial recruiting firms in the United States. In this capacity, Tom has recruited actuaries exclusively since 1996. Tom has worked closely with both clients and candidates at all levels and in across product areas. A few years ago, Tom recognized the need to write this book after reviewing postings on popular actuarial discussion pages. Even though Tom had spent years discussing career choices with actuaries and actuarial students, he was surprised and troubled by the sheer magnitude of misinformation posted on these websites. While actuaries and actuarial students posting this information are trying to be helpful to one another, they frequently lack the necessary experience and/or perspective to offer sound advice. So in spare moments, Tom began working on this book.

The Author's Goal

Tom's goal for this book is to serve as a career resource for actuarial students and credentialed actuaries as they progress through their careers. It is an ambitious goal. Tom recognizes that with this first edition, he has further to go. In the months ahead, the range of topics will be expanded. In fact, a number of these new sections are already in outline or draft form. New versions will become available in both soft cover print for a fee and in PDF form free of charge on Pinnacle Group's website www.pinnaclejobs.com.

Reader Feedback & Questions

Tom expects to update the book periodically. There are a number of topics that Tom expects to write over the next year, but he hopes that the best suggestions for new topics will come from his readers. Constructive feedback will be woven into future editions. Don't be shy. Help Tom aid you and others in the profession by emailing him at info@pinnaclejobs.com. In addition, actuarial career advice questions will be responded to as promptly as possible.

A Recognized Bias

Tom will be the first to acknowledge that he cannot escape his recruiter bias. He is an actuarial recruiter and therefore recognizes the value that recruiters provide to both candidates and clients. With this said, you will see that Tom has made every effort to give advice that can be used by anyone in the industry regardless of how they decide to approach job searches during their careers.

Forward

I have chosen to write this book as a way of helping actuarial students and actuaries with many of the basics of their career decisions. After 17 years of recruiting actuaries, I feel that too few actuaries understand the market for their services and therefore too often make sub-optimal career choices. It is my hope that the first edition of this book will begin raising the awareness of its readers to issues that should be fully considered when making career related decisions. For many of you, I hope it will serve as a useful resource you can repeatedly turn to for assistance as you travel your career paths.

For the most part, the comments in this book are focused on the U.S. employment market, as that is where most of my recruiting expertise is focused. However, I expect that most of the comments translate to non-US markets as well. It is written from the perspective of a "headhunter" and, while cynics may be critical, it's important to recognize that it is also written from the perspective of an expert in the employment market for actuaries. It is nearly impossible for an actuary to have the labor market perspective that a recruiter has for the industry. Knowing the actuarial job market is what we do for a living. What skills are employers looking for and why? How are compensation, benefits and relocation reimbursement expenses changing and why? Where is employment demand the greatest and why? What are the tradeoffs between a career as a pension consultant versus a commercial lines actuary? These are topics that we deal with everyday and the answers to which are found within the pages of this book. While all recruiters may not universally share my opinions, I think that you will recognize the benefits of the information contained within.

Finally, as noted above, I will periodically update the book with new information and I welcome your feedback, suggestions or questions to info@pinnaclejobs.com.

All the best in your career!

Tom Miller
Principal
Pinnacle Group
tom@pinnaclejobs.com

Acknowledgments

I would like to thank the following individuals for their contributions over the years. My first debt of gratitude goes to Nancy Ryan. Before leaving Pinnacle Group in 2005, Nancy and I worked to get this off the ground. Nancy helped outline the book's original framework, provided information for several of the early sections and served as an early editor of the material. Secondly, I'd like to thank both Victoria Cole and Andrea Manning who reviewed and edited large sections of this book. Both Victoria and Andrea provided me with many helpful suggestions that greatly improved the finished product. And finally, I'd like to thank my entire staff for their dedication to Pinnacle Group, our clients and the thousands of candidates who they serve.

1

ABOUT THE ACTUARIAL PROFESSION

Career Overview

What is an actuary?

An actuary is typically defined as an insurance professional who is responsible for creating, modifying, and interpreting a broad range of financial models, data and reports related to insurance products or employee benefits. Most often, actuaries are employed by insurance companies or consulting firms to manage and perform functions related to product pricing and development, establishing and monitoring reserves, managing corporate risk, financial forecasting and financial reporting. As a result, most medium to large insurance companies have sizeable actuarial staffs. In addition, insurance and other large employers may engage actuarial consultants to help them manage, analyze and modify their employee benefits as well as assist with any number of special projects such as risk management or new product creation.

What skills are needed? What degree?

Actuarial work is very technical and requires a strong aptitude for mathematics and statistics. A high percentage of actuarial students enter the profession with undergraduate degrees in mathematics, statistics, engineering or actuarial science. However, these types of degrees are certainly not required. Actuaries come to the profession from nearly every degree imaginable. Many people transition to the profession after several years in a different field and hence their math skills are often rusty as they begin learning the material for the first exams. No matter what your background, employers are much more interested in reviewing your actuarial examination history than what you studied in school. So, the employee with a Ph.D. in Mathematics who has difficulty or cannot pass exams MLC or MFE is going to be less attractive to employers than the candidate with a B.A. in Art History who has passed each of the first four exams on his or her first attempt (all other things being equal).

Why is it a great career?

The actuarial career is regularly rated by business publications, such as *Forbes*, as one of the best careers in the U.S. Why? The short answer is favorable supply and demand characteristics. Actuaries are in short supply relative to the demand by employers. This leads to a high level of employment security and relatively high compensation levels. In today's employment market it is hard to ask for much more than that.

The most recent economic downturn spared very few industries and companies. We all read the headlines about blue chip companies such as Bank of America, General Motors, Nokia, and H-P announcing layoffs of thousands of employees. Insurance companies, particularly life insurance companies, struggled mightily as well. The widespread and steep drop in nearly all asset classes during the "great recession" led to portfolio losses at these and other insurance companies. The most extreme example, of course, was AIG and the historic government bailout needed to cover enormous losses incurred by the firm's financial products unit. AIG and dire headlines aside, actuaries were mostly spared. Actuarial layoffs were higher than in years past, but overall, most actuaries continue to be secure in their positions despite continued economic struggles. The reason, mentioned previously, is supply and demand. The need for actuaries within these companies is still significant and it is simply too difficult to hire enough qualified actuaries for most companies to lay off actuarial staff.

I think of actuaries as the "hub" in the "hub and spoke" organizational structure of an insurance company. Actuaries are central to the success of any insurance company. They develop/revise the products and establish/account for the reserves. Nothing is more central to an insurance company. All other areas of the insurance company from sales, underwriting, marketing, compliance, finance, and administration are the "spokes" that take (and give) direction from the work of actuaries. Of course, each of those non-actuarial functions is critical to the successful operation of any insurance company, but it all starts with the product. And the product, a financial liability or obligation to pay if a particular event happens, is created by the actuarial staff. As a result, compensation for actuarial professionals is quite attractive. Entry-level salaries begin at approximately $45,000 and six-figure compensation is expected for most actuaries who have achieved Fellowship.

Unfortunately, as most of you already know, the difficulty of the exam process makes becoming an actuary very challenging. This is something that *Forbes* magazine fails to mention! For those outside of the profession, I compare the actuarial exam process to law school graduates sitting for the bar exam every six months for 5 to 10 years. It requires an enormous amount of time and energy with no guarantee of success. It bears mentioning that it takes the typical actuarial student 5-10 years to achieve Fellowship. Of course, many do not achieve Fellowship. Many actuarial students stop at the Associate-level and others have successful careers with little or no exam progress. This book will not attempt to address the academic rigors required to pass actuarial exams but will examine career options traditionally open to actuaries as well as prospects for individuals seeking an alternative to the traditional exam path.

Today's Employment Market

Business today is very fast paced. Change is constant and the insurance industry is no exception. The insurance industry, in particular, is very competitive with nearly 4,000 insurance companies in the U.S, many owned by the same parent companies. These companies are constantly offering new products, revising their strategies and reassessing their risks. This has led to employment growth in the insurance industry overall and it has led to greater career opportunities for actuaries in particular. Actuaries work for a variety of employers, including:

- Insurance / Reinsurance Companies
- Consulting / Accounting Firms
- Federal / State Government Agencies & Insurance Depts.
- Banks / Investment Companies
- Fortune 1000 Companies
- Software Development Firms
- Insurance Brokers

Approximately 80% of actuaries work at either insurance companies (including reinsurers) or in consulting (including accounting firms). All other areas of actuarial employment represent relatively small niche areas within the field. Actuarial employment in all of the above areas listed is growing (modestly), except perhaps in the government sector.

Most U.S. actuaries work on the East Coast, Midwest, Texas or California. The reason for this is that most insurance companies and other large employers are located in these states. Therefore, most consulting firms set up offices close to their clients or potential clients. U.S. metropolitan areas with significant pools of actuaries include:

- New York
- Chicago
- Boston
- Philadelphia
- Los Angeles/Orange County
- San Francisco
- Dallas/Ft. Worth
- Minneapolis/St. Paul
- Hartford
- Atlanta
- Baltimore/Washington DC

I stress "metropolitan areas" because often these companies are located in the suburbs of the major cities and not the downtown areas. The two largest markets of New York and Chicago are two very good examples of this geographic spread. Actuarial employment in the suburbs of these two cities is far greater than in the cities themselves. If your city is not listed above, don't despair. If your city has a "major professional sports team" then it's likely to also have a somewhat smaller, but thriving actuarial employment market. Examples include Cincinnati, Charlotte, Houston, Denver and Indianapolis.

Finally, as will be discussed later in the book, pension actuaries typically have greater geographic flexibility than most other actuaries. If you have to work in a small city such as Syracuse, Albuquerque, Salt Lake City, or Knoxville, you're much more likely to find employment at a small benefits consulting firm than at an insurance company.

Actuaries by Product / Specialty Area

As previously mentioned, actuaries have very high job security because employers find it difficult to hire enough qualified actuaries. This difficulty stems, in great part, from the specialization that all actuaries pursue very early in their careers. For now it's enough to point out that there are health actuaries, life/annuity actuaries, pension actuaries, commercial lines actuaries, personal lines actuaries, etc. Each "type" of actuary has very specific skills, knowledge and training. And for reasons discussed later in the book, actuaries typically stay employed within one or two primary product areas throughout their careers. So very early in your career, whether you know it or not, you will be making a choice (actively or passively) about what "type" of actuary you are going to be.

Trends in the U.S Insurance Industry and Their Impact on the Actuarial Profession

The U.S. insurance industry is vast. It provides coverage for a broad array of risks and uses including as investment vehicles (e.g., annuities and GICs). Each major product area (life, health, retirement, personal lines, commercial lines) within the broader insurance industry has its own set of factors impacting it on a daily basis. These are important issues but are normally played out under the broader umbrella of themes, which impact the industry globally. The major issues and trends facing the insurance industry as a whole are:

- Economic weakness and low interest rate environment
- Industry consolidation and cost reduction.
- Continued catastrophes
- Patient Protection and Affordable Care Act
- Tiered pricing
- Underwriting discipline

As with all professions, the actuarial profession is impacted by the industries that it serves. As a result of issues and trends influencing these industries, actuaries are facing new challenges and opportunities as well as more day-to-day performance pressure. While this is the norm in many industries, it is fairly new to actuarial departments and so we will discuss it below.

The Economic Downturn and Low Interest Rates

The financial crisis of 2008 and the ripple effects felt throughout the global economy in the years following are still impacting the insurance industry on many levels. Insurers saw their substantial investment portfolios hit hard by volatility in the financial markets- losses significant enough that portfolios will take years to recover, and which necessitated new approaches to portfolio risk management. State and Federal regulatory environments have become far more complex, requiring insurers to make substantial changes to their operating models to provide for greater transparency and more stringent approaches to risk management at the enterprise level. The effects of the Solvency II legislation in the EU as well as the upcoming NAIC Solvency Modernization Initiative (SMI) in the US have also required insurers to take critical looks at their capital risk management. In effect, a new risk management industry was born and it has changed the inner workings of any and all insurance companies. The new enterprise risk focused environment has most certainly impacted actuarial staffs in a positive way as it has brought actuarial analysis of risk to the forefront of discussion at many companies. (It has also opened up a new career path!)

To quote *The Economist* (April, 2013) "Never in recent economic history have interest rates been so low for so many for so long." While this may be good for you as you look to refinance a mortgage, recent years of historically low rates coupled with expectations that this environment will continue in the coming years have created substantial challenges for insurers who can no longer rely on investment income for profit. Life insurance companies, in particular, are large institutional investors in the market and the low interest rate environment unquestionably altered their business models. Continued product innovation from their actuarial staffs will be necessary to help drive revenues and profits higher.

Industry Consolidation and Cost Reduction

While merger and acquisition activity in the insurance industry dropped off in 2012, the industry is clearly moving toward larger players with bigger balance sheets. Large firms, it is argued, give these companies greater access to investment capital needed to compete effectively in the global and/or the North American marketplace. Industry consolidation has also led to aggressive cost cutting measures, which directly affect all insurance professionals. As an actuary at an insurance company, this industry-wide cost cutting pressure has been counter-balanced by the favorable supply-demand characteristics in the profession. But the drive to cut costs and improve employee productivity is greater today than in years past. This is also a trend at mutual companies and "not-for-profit" health plans but the cost pressure is typically not as intense. Given today's economic environment and the politics of insurance coverage, we see no signs of this pressure abating. As a result, actuarial staffing departments are being stretched (or perhaps consolidated with other actuarial operations) and therefore actuaries are generally working longer hours with somewhat greater resistance to wage increases.

Globalization is here to stay and companies such as these are actively looking to acquire companies or blocks of business that fit their strategic vision and divest units which do not fit their strategy or that are underperforming. The reasons for this are obvious: improved economies of scale and/or improve product/distribution focus. Its impact has been less obvious taken as a whole but quite disruptive to those who are affected by the consolidation of operations. Again, because of the strong demand for actuarial skills, actuaries and actuarial students directly affected by M&A activity have typically been able to find new employment opportunities relatively quickly.

Continued Catastrophes

While we often don't like to think about it in this manner, catastrophes and unforeseen events can be good for the actuarial profession. As experts in risk calculation and risk sharing, your services are needed even more during periods of uncertainty and change than when all is "status quo". This is why when insurance and reinsurance companies face large losses as a result of a change in or perceived change in the underlying aspects of the business environment, they sometimes look to add additional actuarial staff. This makes perfect sense when you compare the potential claims liabilities from a single category 5 hurricane with the cost of additional actuarial staff and improved catastrophe modeling capabilities.

2012 will be remembered by insurers as the year of Superstorm Sandy. Sandy brought devastation to the East Coast of the US, and an estimated $75 billion in damages, making it the second costliest storm in our country's history. It is important to highlight that, while Sandy was the most notable storm, the years 2011 and 2012 saw unprecedented hurricane and tornado activity in the US and had already impaired operating earnings of major property and casualty carriers. 2012 was the costliest year since 2005 when the insurers reeled from the losses incurred by Hurricane Katrina. Costs from Sandy slowed down what was an improving pricing market for insurers in mid 2012.

The continued volume and scope of these catastrophic storms has escalated political debate and scientific discourse on the effects of climate change, and this is a real issue facing insurers today. Actuarial departments will face challenges of how to model catastrophic risk, as well as human health risk as a result of global climate change. The SOA, CAS and AAA have created joint committees to research and assess risk management issues arising from global climate change. As mentioned above, these unfortunate events create interesting professional challenges and opportunities for talented actuaries to be at the forefront of development and implementation of strategy in insurance companies.

Patient Protection and Affordable Care Act

A discussion of healthcare cannot be held at present without reference to the Patient Protection and Affordable Care Act of 2010 (PPACA.) The PPACA is the most sweeping healthcare reform legislation in the United States since the creation of Medicare and Medicaid and is already having a vast impact on the health insurance industry. The legislation is widespread in scope and complex in implementation, which has insurers (and many other stakeholders) struggling to ascertain how to interpret it into their business operations and practices. A significant portion of the legislation takes effect on January 1, 2014 and as a result, 2014 will be a watershed year for health insurers. There will inevitably be unforeseen areas of expense as well as potential revenue streams that arise from the act, and actuaries will play a role in management of each. The PPACA will certainly revolutionize how healthcare is administered and delivered in this country and we can expect the health insurance industry to undergo significant change in the coming years.

The PPACA will also impact casualty carriers, but just how remains to be seen. The number of people with health insurance will rise, and if those people are able to receive care earlier as a result of being insured, both malpractice liability and workers compensations claims could potentially be reduced. At the same time, there will be more insureds overall, yielding potentially more risk for nearly all types of claims. Actuaries will be critical to ensure that rates and reserves are adjusted as necessary when the legislation is implemented in 2014.

Movement Toward Tiered Pricing

One of the basic principles of insurance is that higher risk policyholders should pay higher rates. To that end, the insurance industry is attempting to further expand its use of "tiered pricing". Tiered pricing is the effort by insurance companies to ascertain their best and worst risk customers and modify their pricing accordingly. Today's data warehousing technology provides actuaries and underwriters with powerful tools with which they can better differentiate the risks inherent with different segments of their markets. Accurately matching risk levels with pricing levels is the "holy grail" of pricing and underwriting.

Of course, regulators and legislators are not always so keen to see the insurance industry "differentiate" between customers. Their agenda is different. Regulatory focus is on "fair" pricing and that will frequently run counter to the wishes of the insurance industry. The issue of "fairness" is politically charged as could be seen in the Hurricane Katrina-impacted states of Louisiana and Mississippi. Regulators and insurers locked horns on a wide range of issues related to rates for property insurance. And for many years now, the use of "credit scores" by the auto insurance industry has been hotly contested by most state regulators and legislatures who have sought to block or restrict its use. Actuarial studies demonstrate that a persons' credit history (how they manage their financial affairs), is an excellent predictor of their likelihood to file an insurance claim. Individuals with a high credit score are statistically less likely than individuals with a low credit score to file a claim. Many regulators, however, contend that the use of credit scoring may not be fair or could be discriminatory to minorities and other protected groups who historically have lower credit ratings.

Despite the controversies, however, the trend toward tiered pricing appears to be moving forward, sometimes with the help of new technology. It regularly requires court and legislative battles, but insurance companies are quite familiar with these arenas. The actuarial profession will be at the forefront of these efforts. After all, it is the goal of actuarial staff at every company to correlate rates for insurance policies as closely as possible with the actual cost of claims. The more accurately they achieve this, the lower the rates for the insureds and the greater the profitability for the insurance company.

Improved Underwriting Discipline

When the stock, bond and real estate markets are booming, the insurance business becomes a lot easier. Underwriting mistakes can easily be forgotten/ forgiven when investments under management produce outsized gains. However, as referenced previously, the US economy is in the midst of a period of historically low interest rates, which puts significant downward pressure on margins for many insurers. As a result, insurers are now looking to every corner of their organizations for new methods of enhancing profitability and many company CEO's have been quoted as saying they are taking a "Back to Basics" approach to profitability. Nothing is more basic or fundamental to an insurer than its underwriting operations and, as such, improved underwriting discipline is a key part of virtually every insurers strategy in this market. Actuaries are critical to the underwriting effort as they are the staff responsible for designing the insurance product pricing to be in line as closely as possible with the actual cost of claims. And while this has always been important, in today's economic environment, it is even more so.

Trends in the Actuarial Employment Market

Favorable Supply vs. Demand Characteristics

Despite continued weakness in the U.S. economy, the prospects for continued long-term strength in the actuarial employment market remain solid. As mentioned earlier, there are not enough college or graduate students pursuing careers in actuarial science after graduation to meet insurance industry demand. Students with strong mathematical skills are highly sought after by a diverse range of industries. This competition for talent has led to fewer students making the decision to undergo the years of studying required to gain professional accreditation as an Associate or Fellow. Even in today's soft job market, the demand for talented actuarial students is greater than the supply. The shortage improves job stability for the profession as a whole. For this reason, even if you read headlines about "layoffs at ABC insurance company", you should recognize that despite the layoffs to other personnel, the company is likely hiring for actuaries or actuarial students.

These favorable supply and demand characteristics are expected to remain in place for many years (if not decades). Moreover, the U.S.'s current immigration policy severely limits the pool of immigrants available to enter the actuarial profession. Due to the added cost and legal paperwork, most employers either refuse entirely or rarely "sponsor" foreign actuaries for employment in this country.

Potential Off Shoring

A Wall Street Journal article from March 28, 2007 listed the actuarial profession as one of the most "highly offshorable". (The article did not discuss the particulars of why the actuarial profession was listed, but instead focused on the changes to the free-trade thinking of Alan S. Blinder, Princeton University economist and former Federal Reserve Board vice chairman.) The Wall Street Journal and Mr. Blinder may not recognize factors that make "offshoring" the actuarial profession more difficult than computer programming, however. For example, the SOA and CAS credentialing processes limit the supply of qualified actuaries in the U.S. The exams administered by these two industry associations are designed to meet the needs of the North American market. U.S. employers therefore require SOA and CAS exams and designations for their employees. Mutual recognition rules between US and the UK, for example, do exist however UK actuaries are not easily placed into the U.S. market as their education and training is fairly different than their American counterparts. This is primarily due to the differences in the insurance markets and regulation in both countries. Nonetheless, some off-shoring is inevitable as globalization continues its unending march.

2

BEGINNING A CAREER
AS AN ACTUARY

Getting Started: Important Criteria

As a recruiting firm, Pinnacle Group receives a large number of emails from aspiring actuarial students worldwide. Regardless of your particular circumstances, our initial response is nearly always the same. Beginning a career as a U.S. actuarial student requires the following three items:

1. Eligibility to work in the U.S. full-time
2. Current primary residence in the U.S.
3. Successful completion of at least one actuarial exam (Exam P/1 or FM/2)

Eligible to Work in the U.S. Full-Time

For most entry-level actuaries, the first follow-up question is often, what do you mean by "eligible to work in the U.S. full-time"? This is a good question. Unfortunately, there are very few "absolutes" when it comes to employers' willingness to hire entry-level actuarial students who do not currently have U.S. citizenship or permanent work visas (H-1B).

Many actuarial students are in the U.S. legally under an F-1 (student) visa. This is fairly common as bright young students from around the world come to U.S. universities to pursue degrees in mathematics, statistics, actuarial science or other fields that lend themselves to a career as an actuary. Under the F-1 visa, your eligibility to work full-time is finite. Employers who wish to hire you must begin the H-1B visa sponsorship process to keep you employed at their firms beyond the 29 month limit. Unfortunately, U.S. immigration policy is not well conceived. For decades, the U.S. has made it very difficult and expensive for employers to hire talented people from around the world who wish to work in this country. The current cap of 85,000 H-1B visas granted each year means that employers find it very difficult to get applications approved for their employees. As a result, many firms have simply chosen not to sponsor any employees for H-1B visas. This is particularly true of companies that do not have an international presence, which unfortunately represents a significant portion of U.S. insurance companies. As a result, if you are living in the U.S. under an F-1 visa, the potential pool of employers is much smaller than if you had your "green card". There are certainly firms willing to sponsor- but it's a small number.

The second point to consider if you are here under an F-1 visa is that you may be at a relative disadvantage as compared to those with permanent work status. All things being equal, hiring an entry-level actuarial student who requires H-1B sponsorship is more difficult and expensive than hiring one who does not require sponsorship. You cannot fight this, you can only be aware of it, and do your best to make sure you are a more attractive candidate with other factors such as your communication skills, exam progress, exam scores, internships, etc.

Living in the U.S.

If you want to work in the U.S., you must be living in the U.S. legally (or perhaps in Canada legally). I stress both living here legally and full-time (not just visiting for a month in an attempt to find a job). You simply will not be able to get a position without these conditions being met. The only exception to this is perhaps with some Canadian actuarial students. A number of companies, typically the large consulting firms, will interview Canadian university students, for opportunities in northern U.S. cities. As a result of NAFTA, employment in the U.S. under a TN visa is a fairly simple process. Despite its ease and low financial cost to employers, however, you will still find a high percentage of employers unwilling to consider Canadian actuarial students. The TN visa is often viewed as a complication and many U.S. companies are simply unwilling to take the extra time necessary to either understand or complete the process required.

If you are living here legally, perhaps under an F-1 visa, then you will find that some employers are willing to sponsor entry-level actuarial students for their green cards. As discussed previously, it is not an easy process attempting to identify the firms willing to sponsor you but it can be done. You will likely find if they do agree to hire you and sponsor you for your green card, that the company may not start the process for six or twelve months after your start date. Companies often want to evaluate your performance before agreeing to begin the laborious and costly green card process.

Finally, if you are living in the U.S. illegally, don't even bother applying for an actuarial position. Even if the company wanted to hire you after completing the interview process, they will almost certainly discover that you are here illegally and the offer, if made, will be immediately rescinded.

Passing Your First Exams

As stated previously, you must have passed at least one actuarial exam (preferably two) to be considered for full-time entry-level actuarial employment. If you have not passed either P/1 or FM/2, again, do not bother applying. It will be a waste of your time as there are too many qualified applicants who will be selected over you. The fact is that you simply do not yet qualify as an actuarial student. Nearly all employers use the one exam passed minimum criteria to weed out applicants that have not taken serious steps toward beginning their actuarial careers. Without an exam passed, you will not be considered by the majority of actuarial employers.

Please note, more is not always better when it comes to exams and obtaining your first full-time position as an actuarial student. In fact, too many exams can work against you. The ideal number is two exams passed, perhaps two plus MFE/3F or MLC/3L. Any more exams passed, and you run the risk of "pricing yourself out of the market". To understand what I mean by this you have to understand how most of the large insurance companies and consulting firms compensate their employees who are part of their actuarial student programs. Actuarial students at these firms are compensated based on a combination of years of experience and exams passed. These two factors are expected to rise together, allowing for greater compensation as both experience and exams passed increase. However, if an entry-level actuarial student has too many exams, this compensation "formula" is broken immediately. It breaks because the exam raises and/or bonuses paid to the actuarial student for passing each exam are typically a matter of fixed policy and not subject to modification. Therefore, an employer may be faced with a situation such as the following: A well-respected actuarial student with three years of service at the firm and three exams passed may be earning $56,000 plus a 5% bonus. While a new hire, with no employment history with the company but having passed the first four exams and Modules 1-5 of FAP would have to be paid $60,000 based solely on exam progress. Most companies won't pay these compensation rates without work experience. They want to hire an entry-level actuarial student at $48,000 to $50,000 and have their compensation gradually increase through the combination of exam progress and experience. Due to the nature of their schooling, there are some Canadian actuarial students who graduate with four exams passed and the market for these candidates is strong- however they are the exception rather than the norm. In general, companies are highly unlikely to pursue the entry-level actuary with four or more exams.

Product Areas: Choosing the Right Line of Business for You

As a new entrant to the actuarial profession, you may not be aware that actuarial work is typically separated into several areas of sub-specialization. Some of this may be obvious to you as you see that there are two organizations in North America that govern distinct areas of the profession (the Society of Actuaries and the Casualty Actuarial Society). These two governing bodies work together on early actuarial education (for now, though this will change at the end of 2013) but the accreditation process is quite distinct between the SOA and the CAS. Moreover, even within the SOA or CAS path, there are areas of sub-specialization that can make significant differences in your career. As noted in the table below, Pinnacle Group typically identifies five major lines of business (aka product areas). Choosing the right line of business for you is particularly important. For reasons I'll discuss below, actuaries do not easily move between sub-specialty areas. Actuaries often develop a line of business expertise early and then remain in the same general product areas for the rest of their careers.

Pinnacle Group estimates there are approximately 25,000 to 30,000 actuaries and actuarial students employed in the U.S. today. Generally speaking the five primary product areas in the US market are as follows:

Product Area	% of US Actuaries [1]
Life & Annuity	26.5
Health & Managed Care (including Disability, LTC, Dental, and Group Life)	25.4
Pension & Retirement Benefits	26.0

Commercial Lines (P&C)	13.9
Personal Lines (P&C)	8.2

(1)   Based on an analysis of the Pinnacle Group database (2/09). Non-actuarial product areas in which an actuary might be working were excluded from this analysis. Reinsurance actuaries were included with the product type they reinsure (e.g., life reinsurance)

All of the above areas offer long careers with plenty of interesting and rewarding actuarial work. As is often the case with most career decisions, there are pluses and minuses with each path. As an entry-level actuarial student, you may be fortunate enough to receive more than one job offer within the actuarial profession. If this is the case, and if the competing offers are with companies that operate in different product areas, you will need to weigh the pros and cons of each opportunity before selecting the firm you'd like to join. Part of that decision will be short-term considerations such as starting base salary, location and benefits. However, when evaluating the long-term prospects of the opportunity, it is more important than you might think to consider "what line of business is right for me"? This is not easy, as you don't know what factors may influence your life in the years ahead but, as with any decision, you must work with the facts presented to you. The important point to remember is that you can't make a wrong decision. The actuarial profession, regardless of your area of sub-specialization, will provide you with terrific opportunities to learn and grow.

To help you make a decision that is most optimal for *you* given your career goals and interests, I've outlined the following three aspects to consider:

1. Product Area Consistency: The product area in which you start your career is likely where you will end your career
2. Marketability & Geography: Your product specialization will impact your ability to change jobs and geographic locations
3. Compensation Potential: Your product specialization will impact your compensation potential

Product Area Consistency

As stated above, the product area in which you start your career is likely where you will end your career. Researching our database, we found that

81% of actuaries stayed within the same product area for their entire career. Furthermore, we found that of those actuaries who did change product area, 45% of them made that change within 2 years of beginning their career and 68% within 5 years.

The data shows that as you advance in your career, the likelihood of switching to a new product area declines significantly. Why is this so? Let's look at this from the employers' point of view first. When companies decide to hire an experienced actuary, they are looking to identify candidates with a proven set of specific skills. The more senior the position, the more true this becomes, and therefore the less flexibility they will show in the hiring process. For example, if the company is hiring an FSA who is expected to manage a staff of five individual annuity pricing actuaries, they will almost certainly seek to hire someone with both individual annuity pricing/product development experience and prior management experience. The employer is expecting to pay this person a six-figure salary plus bonus and will not want to settle for someone under-qualified. They don't want to hire an FSA with life pricing and management experience, for example; or a technically strong annuity pricing actuary who has no experience managing a staff. They want to hire someone who can join their organization as an expert, lead the staff and "hit the ground running". If the role allowed for less then they would be more likely to promote from within the organization. They could pay less for the position and give a junior annuity pricing actuary an opportunity to step up into a managerial role. However, in this case they've chosen to go outside the company to find a candidate who meets their parameters.

Adding to employers' reluctance to hire under-qualified applicants are today's lean corporate structures and fast-paced business marketplaces. Corporate budgets are tighter than ever and this has led many companies (not just insurance companies) to cut back on training and development of their staff. Training is expensive and costs employers both dollars and time. This is true whether the training is formal classroom instruction or on-the-job training, allowing someone to gain experience in a new area. Adding to this cost is high employee turnover as numerous studies show that today's employees feel less allegiance to their employers than they did in decades past. So understandably, even at the most junior levels, companies look to hire individuals with "day one" expertise. They don't want to have you learning a new position for six or more months only to leave in two years. They'd rather hire someone who can make an immediate impact. There are lower costs and less risk with an experienced hire. This is a trend we have seen become stronger year over year particularly in a weak economic environment.

From the employee's perspective it typically makes sense to stay within the same product area as well. Once you begin working in a particular product area, you are investing in your career and developing expertise in that specialty. Over time, your employer's recognition of your growing expertise and contribution to the firm will begin increasing your compensation and responsibilities. For most individuals, it will make sense to continue along this path; to build upon your existing skill sets and be rewarded for doing so. This is what drives your career growth. And for all the reasons listed above, it is easier to convince a prospective new employer of your worth if you have a proven track record in a particular product area. A career switch from life products to managed care products, for example, requires "starting over" to a large degree. As noted previously, most employers will not be interested to hire you in such instances. However, in those cases where they do entertain hiring you, they will almost always discount your previous experience as not relevant to the current opening. As a result, you may face a pay cut or a position of lower responsibility.

Finally, there is the issue of exams. As of the writing of this book, no discussion of exams can occur without mention of the SOA's plans to discontinue joint preliminary exams with the CAS as of December 31, 2013. While the CAS has indicated it will continue to recognize early SOA exams for credit towards CAS designations, this impending split will likely contribute to further specialization by product earlier on, though the impact may not be too significant.

Companies already look for directly relevant experience first and foremost when they hire, making it difficult for even junior level actuarial students to leave their current product areas. To illustrate, if you have two candidates pursuing one P&C opening; one with 3 exams passed and 2 years of Life product experience and another with 2 exams passed and 2 years of P&C experience, all other things equal, the second candidate is most likely to be hired. This is particularly true if there are multiple P&C candidates being considered and you are the only Life candidate submitted for the position.

Product Specialization and its Impact on Marketability and Geography

It may not seem obvious at the outset of your career but your area of product specialization, or sub-specialization, will impact your marketability and your geographic flexibility throughout your career. The impact of these differences can be significant depending upon your career goals. I'll discuss the pros and cons of each product area as it relates to "marketability" (or the ease of finding new employment) and geographic flexibility but for now, I'll simply state the following: the more specialized your product area and the fewer people with those skills available, the higher your compensation may be (based on simple supply and demand) and the greater geographic flexibility you may need to secure new employment in the same product area.

To illustrate, let's review marketability and geographic flexibility for pension versus a very specialized commercial lines actuary. The responsibilities of a typical pension actuary are fairly similar, generally speaking, across all pension consulting firms. Of course, there are many individual differences based upon the clients of the firm but the products are normally defined benefit plans and the clients are typically medium to large employers. Your pension actuarial skills are very transferrable and therefore, easily marketable to a wide number of firms. Given the fact that pension clients (and therefore pension consulting firms serving those clients) are essentially located in every good-sized city in the U.S., you have geographic flexibility to move across the country or across town to do similar work. The commercial lines actuary who specializes in environmental liability, however, faces a very different marketplace for his skills. There are far fewer companies in the U.S. that offer environmental liability products. These companies are often located in only the largest U.S. cities. It is not likely that you'll find them in smaller cities such as Columbus, Pittsburgh, Washington D.C., St. Louis, Denver, Portland, Omaha, etc. Yet, all of these cities have sizeable populations of pension actuaries. The point being, if you are a highly specialized actuary who needs or wants to change his/her job, your only option may be to relocate to a new city to find suitable employment. This is important to consider given that your actuarial career may span 40 years.

Product Specialization May Impact Your Compensation

Continuing with the illustration above, supply and demand factors are clearly in your favor as a specialized commercial lines actuary when it comes to compensation. Generally speaking, commercial lines actuaries are the most highly paid actuaries in the U.S. Over time, they will be better paid than defined benefit (and most other types of) actuaries with the same number of exams, years of experience, etc. but, as noted above, it will come at a cost to their geographic flexibility. Why is this so? Why aren't personal lines actuaries paid similarly, for example? The reason rests squarely on the depth of sub-specialization that most commercial lines actuaries acquire during their careers. Commercial lines products cover an enormous array of risks from aviation, property and liability, workers' compensation, directors & officers, and medical malpractice, just to name a small fraction of coverages. Personal lines actuaries, on the other hand, typically work on a much smaller range of risks, generally falling into two primary areas: personal auto and homeowners. Employers needing an environmental liability actuary have a more difficult time finding a qualified applicant and compensation rises as a result.

Please keep in mind that the differences in compensation are often fairly modest. Over time, compensation falls squarely on individual performance. If you are successful as an actuary, you will earn six-figure compensation regardless of the path you choose. Earning more money in your career is directly related to your innate talent, willingness to work hard and make sacrifices that put your career first. If you are willing to put in longer hours and take the initiative to move up the corporate ladder, and if you are willing to invest in your career and seek out opportunities that pay more and provide growth opportunities, you will be well compensated regardless of what product area (Life, Health, Pension, P&C) you choose.

Product Areas: Overview

Assuming you sleep 8 hours per night and work 40 hours per week, you spend 36% of your waking hours as an adult at work. To me that means that you had better enjoy both what you do and where you work. If you don't, you may want to consider an employment change because life goes by too quickly. You are also far more likely to excel in a field that you are passionate about.

Number of Hours Worked Per Week	% of Waking Hours	Number of Hours Worked Per Week	% of Waking Hours
35	30%	60	52%
40	36%	65	56%
45	39%	70	60%
50	43%	75	65%
55	47%	80	69%

Which product area to work in may be one of your first career decisions. In an ideal world, as graduating undergraduate or graduate student, you will have multiple offers from a number of companies. During the on-campus recruiting process, you will get valuable information directly from the companies about the opportunities that exist at these firms. But a broader, recruiter-perspective on the various product areas can be valuable even at this early stage.

For the purpose of simplification, I will treat "multi-line" insurance companies as completely separate entities. Multi-line companies are typically defined as insurance holding companies that underwrite and market both Life & Annuity and P&C products. Each subsidiary is a wholly separate entity and as such, actuaries in one or the other subsidiaries almost never have the opportunity to switch between companies (even though they share the same parent). The same is true of consulting firms. If you start out in the P&C area, for example, it is very unlikely that you would be moved to the pension or life areas.

Life & Annuity

Overview

Life insurance companies offer a wide range of products including life, annuity, disability, and long-term care products. An actuarial career in the life insurance industry can be diverse and rewarding. It spans both individual and group products and includes non-medical products such as disability, group life and long-term care. The market is dominated by large insurers with sizeable actuarial staffs that are more likely to offer traditional rotational student programs. But there is plenty of room for the thousands of smaller U.S. life insurance companies that focus on a particular market(s) or geography. Careers at these smaller companies can be very attractive as well.

When the general population thinks of life insurance, they tend to think of a standard "term life" policy. These policies have been sold for decades and they appear quite simple. If you die during the term of the policy, your beneficiaries collect the face value of the policy. But the actuarial assumptions behind these policies are far more complex and require constant re-analysis. Today, life insurance products have become significantly more diverse and complex. The industry has stepped forward with a mindboggling number of creative life insurance and annuity products designed to meet consumers' changing insurance and investment needs. And while the life insurance market may not be on the front page of the newspapers as frequently as say "health insurance" or "homeowners insurance" the market is just as vibrant and exciting as any sub-sector of the actuarial field.

As with many insurance products, work in the actuarial areas of life & annuity companies tends to be focused on pricing/product development or valuation (reserves)/financial reporting. Pricing/product development is focused on the creation and/or modification of insurance products for segments of the marketplace. Product pricing work is critical because it is largely responsible for profitability and therefore the ultimate success or failure of the product. A huge amount of analysis and complex modeling supports pricing work including analysis of existing products, policyholder experience studies, competition, intra-company requirements (e.g., return on equity), administration and other expenses, and regulatory factors. It is an ever-changing environment and requires regular re-evaluation once the products are introduced into the marketplace. Of paramount consideration are always the reserves and the valuation and financial reporting of those reserves by the actuaries. Simply stated, reserves are monies set aside to pay future claims by policyholders. Calculating reserves is complex work that requires sophisticated models, which analyze reserves in a multitude of ways. It is as much art as science and must be done regularly to satisfy both internal and external audiences (shareholders and regulatory bodies.) Finally, there are a number of other roles that actuaries play within a life insurance company including asset-liability modeling, corporate level analysis, and research/special projects. There is no shortage of work, as a tremendous amount of actuarial analysis needs to be continuously undertaken.

Benefits

Working as an actuary or actuarial student at a life and annuity insurance company often offers the benefits of a large company with many opportunities for diverse work experience and upward mobility. While not all life insurers are large, consolidation in the life insurance industry has led to fewer firms accounting for an ever greater percentage of actuarial hiring than in years past. Larger companies will more likely offer structured, rotational actuarial student programs. These programs provide actuarial students with the opportunity to rotate through different departments and product areas before settling into a specialty. Rotations are not necessary at smaller insurance companies. Due to their smaller staff size, actuaries are almost always given broader product or functional responsibilities. Large or small, both are attractive options and both can lead to careers in either senior management (within an insurance company) or consulting. However, the career differences early on will differ and should be considered.

Actuarial consultants are often used by life and annuity insurance companies. The range of consulting projects is typically quite diverse and cutting edge. Often they will focus on actuarial projects that the client's current staff either does not have expertise in, such as developing a new variable life product, or does not have time for, such as quarterly or annual valuation and financial reporting support.

Considerations:

Individual (as opposed to group) life and annuity products are the core products marketed by most life insurance companies. As such, it is preferable to get individual life insurance and/or annuity actuarial experience if you work for one of these companies. (Generally speaking, it is always preferable to get experience working in the "core product area" of your industry as it increases your employment marketability.) A study of our Pinnacle Group database shows that actuarial employment directly related to individual life and annuity products represents approximately 85-90% of the employment opportunities available at life insurance companies. Group life, group annuity and other group non-medical products therefore represent only between 10-15% of actuarial employment opportunities. This means that you will have greater employment flexibility in your career if you have individual life or annuity products experience.

Up to 15% of "life" actuaries work with either individual or group "non-medical" products such as Short- and Long-Term Disability Income (DI), Group Life, Long-Term Care and other specialty products such as Critical Illness, etc. This is still a very sizable segment of the market and generally gives actuaries enough geographic and employment flexibility to remain within this product area without undue concern if opportunities within individual life and annuity do not materialize or you find you prefer working with these products. But, it is important that you regularly assess your career and your desire for specialization. If you have 12 years of group DI experience and want to or need to change positions, it can be challenging without major geographic concessions. At any given time, there simply may not be enough open positions at your level and/or close to the geography that you prefer, if you specialize in a product that is not widely marketed.

Retirement/Pension & Health Benefits

Overview

The retirement/pension and health benefits product areas are largely the domain of consulting firms that serve the retirement, healthcare and other benefits needs of medium to large-sized employers. Broadly speaking, companies use actuarial/benefits consulting firms to:

- Develop strategies to achieve their staffing goals (employee attraction and retention)
- Develop strategies to achieve their financial goals (employee benefits cost containment)
- Adhere to federal and state laws governing employee benefits

As a benefits actuary, you will almost certainly be working in the retirement area (defined benefit, defined contribution and retiree medical) or the health area (medical insurance products and group non-medical products such as group disability, group life, group long-term care). Regardless of the area in which you work, most benefits consultants are involved in plan valuations and plan design among many other possible functions. The market opportunity for consulting firms is to make sure that they help their clients achieve their goals as they relate to employee benefits and do so in a manner that is fiscally responsible and in compliance with various state and federal laws.

Benefits

There are many advantages to being a pension/benefits actuary but perhaps the greatest is the geographic flexibility that the specialty provides. Benefits actuarial firms are in every corner of the U.S. This is not true of insurance companies or the firms that consult to them.

Historically, the consulting industries have enjoyed steady employment growth leading to stability in employment. From 2008 through to today, however we have observed benefits consulting firms adding only selective staff and some modest layoffs have been made at several firms. We observed a similar level of employment activity in 2002 after the events of 9/11 froze the world for nearly a year. In general though, the benefits consulting market is better insulated from economic swings than many other industries. This is true in part because in good times and bad, firms are constantly reassessing their benefits strategies and responding to changes in the law.

Another consideration is that you can become a benefits consultant without the pressure to necessarily pursue actuarial exams. Actuarial Consultants at benefits consulting firms are focused on technical, actuarial analysis, which by its nature is the cornerstone of the work provided. But you needn't be an actuary to be a benefits consultant. Benefits consultants typically have a financial background with strong analytical skills but they are not responsible for actuarial work. Nor are they required to have graduate degrees in finance or other related fields. So if you are unsure about pursuing actuarial exams, benefits consulting may provide an alternate track for you to follow without changing careers. As a benefits consultant you are just as likely to serve as a lead consultant or project manager for clients and projects as an Actuarial Consultant. And you'll be just as likely to manage and/or work with large complex teams that span multiple geographic locations. Your focus will be on such things as managing benefit plan cost analyses, financial projections and renewal negotiations, competitive plan benchmarking, health and group product marketing, employee cost-sharing strategies (design, pricing, and implementation), care management (design, pricing, and implementation), vendor and performance management, preparing proposals and identifying new business opportunities with existing clients and expanding relationships.

A few additional advantages to benefits consulting are as follows: For those actuaries pursuing an investment track, pension actuarial may be slightly more likely lead to asset-side investment positions if desired. In addition, later in your career, pension consulting can lead to entrepreneurial endeavors for those who decide to "hang their own shingle" and pursue smaller clients.

Considerations

Consulting often means travel, especially as you advance in your career. This may not be for everyone and can become tiresome over the years. Consulting is a client-driven, "client comes first" atmosphere that some people thrive on and others do not. It can be very exciting and expose you to a wide variety of projects. It can also put added pressures on people, including actuarial students, who may prefer a more structured environment with well-defined functional responsibilities.

Consulting positions can also mean less exam study time. That being said, consulting firms want their actuarial students to pass their exams and they typically do their best to see that their actuarial students get their allotted study time. What often differs from an insurance company atmosphere is the flexibility as to when you get your study time. In consulting, you may find that you cannot take time off to study when you prefer. You will find that you have to work with your manager and select study days that reflect the needs of the office and its clients. This is not all that different from an insurance company except that the consulting environment necessitates aligning your study time with the needs of the client and that typically creates more upheaval in one's study schedule. An insurance company atmosphere is often more predictable, though I'm sure you can find plenty of students who would disagree. In recognition of this issue, all the major actuarial consulting firms seek to hire actuarial students with proven exam passing skills. Their view is that if they hire the best exam passers, that they will continue to progress despite the challenges presented by a client-driven atmosphere.

You may also wish to consider the size of the firm or the office that you work for. Smaller firms/offices tend to provide a wider variety of work than larger firms/offices. For example, as an actuarial consultant in Charlotte you may work on both retirement and health benefits while your counterparts in New York and Chicago will most likely be specialized in one or the other. It's worth noting however, that larger offices do offer considerable project variety within specialty areas so both can be equally rewarding.

One final consideration is that pension actuaries are often expected to pass even more exams! While arguably not as difficult as the SOA or CAS exams, the Enrolled Actuary (EA) exams do add travel time to your efforts to attain professional accreditation. The SOA, the American Society of Pension Professionals and Actuaries (ASPPA), and the Joint Board for the Enrollment of Actuaries (JBEA) co-sponsor and administer two actuarial examinations that must be successfully completed to obtain your Enrolled Actuary designation. For current information regarding these exams, I suggest you visit the ASPPA website (www.asppa.org).

Fortunately, some of the material overlaps with the SOA and/or undergraduate studies so you may receive waivers for part of the EA-1 exam depending upon your SOA exam progress. Rules for waivers change often so again you'll want to visit the ASPPA website for the most current details.

Health/Managed Care

Overview

Healthcare insurance in the U.S. is a challenging endeavor, and as such it can be very interesting work. The Healthcare/Managed Care industry covers a wide range of products and companies, and your flexibility to move between the different areas during your career is relatively high. The healthcare universe includes the following diverse opportunities:

- Insurance Companies
  - "Blues" Plans (Group and/or Individual)
  - HMOs/Managed Care Companies (Group primarily)
  - Individual Health Products
- Reinsurance (Group and/or Individual)
- Consulting (Group and/or Individual Health)
  - Employer Benefits
  - Provider & Insurance

Over time, you will begin to develop expertise in either group (marketed through employers) or individual products. Within group health, you may also begin to specialize in small or large group insurance. Regardless of your choice, you are unlikely to face significant barriers to moving within the health arena. A high percentage of health actuaries do move within their specialty area during their careers. That being said, there are wide differences between how group and individual products are priced, for example, and our clients typically prefer certain skills for certain positions. Those candidates that most closely match the position description will be interviewed first and be the most likely hired. Experience does count. And the more senior the position, the more clients will require a particular skill set.

As a healthcare actuary, you will most likely be involved in pricing/product development, experience/claims analysis or loss reserves analysis. This work gets right to the heart of the healthcare debate that is raging across the nation. As with most actuarial work, it is quite challenging with a lot of moving parts. Of course, U.S. healthcare is a lightening rod for media attention; so prepare to hear lots of unsolicited advice (i.e., complaints) from people who have strong opinions on the topic!

Benefits

As stated above, a career as a health actuary typically gives its practicing actuaries fairly significant career choice and geographic flexibility. As a health actuary, you have opportunities to work with health insurance companies including "Blues Plans" (Blue Cross/Blue Shield organizations), stand alone HMOs, and reinsurance companies. In addition, there are a large number of firms that provide health care consulting services. Only pension actuaries enjoy more geographic flexibility.

Considerations

One of the most salient characteristics of the health care industry has been its profitability challenges. Generally speaking, managed care has not "managed" to consistently achieve profitability targets. This is due to a myriad of reasons beyond the scope of this book and beyond the expertise of its author. Needless to say, participants in the healthcare industry have turned to actuaries to help them analyze and react to the factors that impact claims and pricing. The PPACA will place even greater scrutiny on industry profitability and cost containment. For this reason, we expect demand to remain strong for healthcare actuaries. Someday, however, profitability issues may impact actuarial employment in a variety of ways including potentially lower compensation and/or lower job security. But for now, and the foreseeable future, the favorable supply and demand characteristics in the employment market for healthcare actuaries is very positive.

Another consideration is that healthcare companies and consulting firms rarely have formal rotational programs (unlike many Life and P&C insurance companies). If you are in provider-side or health insurance consulting, you are likely getting quite a variety of project work (making the idea of a rotation basically moot). Typically, however, actuarial students in the healthcare industry must take a more proactive role in managing their career development. Of course, that is something we recommend for all actuarial professionals.

Finally, it is important as a health actuary to get group healthcare experience. Group insurance is the most popular commercial health insurance coverage in the U.S. You should attempt to gain this experience at your earliest opportunity. Group health experience will give you more employment flexibility than experience with individual health insurance because group health actuarial jobs outnumber individual health jobs, approximately 4 to 1 (Source: Pinnacle Group database analysis, 2/12/09). As your career develops, the type of group experience quickly becomes important, principally classified as either Large Group or Small Group experience. There are many companies that specialize in products designed for either large employer groups or small employer groups and many that offer products for both. As you progress in your career, specialization in one or the other may begin to limit your career options. There are significant differences in the pricing for each market segment. Often it is best if you have experience with both at some point in your career and at a level of sufficient responsibility as to matter to prospective employers.

Property & Casualty

Overview

Property & Casualty work is commonly divided into two primary product areas, personal lines and commercial lines. Personal lines products are focused on individual's property insurance needs, most notably, automobile and homeowners insurance. Commercial lines products are focused on the needs of businesses, not-for-profits, governments and other commercial interests.

Most personal lines actuaries work for insurance companies specializing in auto and homeowners insurance. Often these companies are the "household" names in insurance (e.g., Allstate, State Farm, Progressive, Geico, etc.) that have large consumer-oriented advertising budgets and cute mascots or catchy jingles (think talking geckos and "You're in good hands with Allstate"). Other common personal lines products include renters insurance, specialty auto (e.g., RV, motorcycle, snowmobile) and "umbrella" or liability insurance that helps protect your assets from lawsuits should someone injure themselves as a result of an automobile or household accident.

Commercial lines products are much more diverse. One might expect this given all of the various types of organizations and their equally disparate insurance needs. Some of the major commercial product categories include property, general liability, workers compensation, commercial auto, professional liability, and transportation insurance. The diversity within commercial lines also drives more opportunities in the area of consulting than personal lines products.

Regardless of personal or commercial lines, the functions performed by P&C actuaries are similar. They include:

- Reserving
- Rating/Pricing
- Modeling/Dynamic Financial Analysis
- Catastrophe Modeling
- Product Management
- Data Mgt/Systems/Programming
- Regional Actuary
- Claims / Experience Analysis

Other common P&C opportunities may include positions in insurance brokerage, reinsurance and work at insurance bureaus. These opportunities all present interesting work but will not be addressed within this book at this time.

Benefits

Generally speaking P&C actuaries are the most highly paid actuaries in the U.S. market. Within P&C, personal lines actuaries tend to focus on more standardized products, such as personal auto and homeowners policies.

As a result, their degree of sub-specialization is typically not as great as that of commercial lines actuaries. The wide spectrum of commercial lines products leads to the largest imbalance of supply and demand in the actuarial employment market. This imbalance has led to historically higher pay for commercial lines actuaries.

Considerations

Commercial lines actuaries, in particular, and personal lines actuaries to a lesser degree, are very specialized. Unfortunately, specialization has a downside. There are fewer employers interested in these skills and they are located in a smaller number of cities than for pension, life or health actuaries. This often results in P&C actuaries making geographic relocations to new cities (when the time comes to make a job change) and/or longer search periods. The likelihood of relocation can be reduced by working in a city with a large P&C employment base such as New York or Chicago. But even in such large metropolitan areas, you may find it somewhat more challenging to find a comparable or better job quickly.

Reinsurance

Overview

Reinsurance is essentially insurance for insurance companies. To assure their long-term financial security, insurance companies need to spread and limit their risk. Reinsurance companies offer the primary means for achieving this goal. Similar to the direct insurance market, you'll find that many reinsurance companies specialize in one or more of the major product areas such as life, health or P&C.

Actuarial work at reinsurance companies differs from work at insurance companies and at consulting firms. In some ways you might say that it blends aspects of both but overall, it is more similar to work at an insurance company. What makes reinsurance different is the nature of the customer. Insurance companies are the reinsurers' customers. Reinsurance actuaries are typically analyzing blocks of business, in aggregate, rather than the separate policyholders. In this role, reinsurance actuaries are often interfacing directly with their actuarial counterparts on the insurance company side. For example, in order for a reinsurance actuary to price a bid on a block of an insurance company's business, they need to understand the actuarial assumptions and risks associated with the block. Communication, actuary to actuary, is commonplace. Both sides of the transaction or potential transaction are very knowledgeable. Much of the same information is being distributed to competing reinsurance companies who are also considering bids on the block of business. It is an interesting and competitive arena with big dollars, profits AND losses, at stake.

Benefits

When big dollars are at stake, work is typically interesting and atmosphere is dynamic. This is certainly true at a reinsurance company. The scope of product pricing is more varied than a pricing role at a primary insurer, and there is less administrative work associated with it. Client exposure typically also comes with a reinsurance role. We hear from reinsurance actuaries that they feel they have a blend of consulting and primary insurance work. As far as compensation goes, upside is typically higher than at an insurance company. The higher upside is usually structured in the form of a larger target annual bonus, so it is not a guaranteed part of compensation. If the company meets its targets, experienced actuaries may find themselves earning bonuses twice that of their peers at primary insurance companies.

Considerations

Unfortunately, reinsurance is a more volatile market than primary insurance, and is less insulated from the booms and busts in a changing economy. With a few years as exceptions, the reinsurance industry has consolidated quite significantly in the last 15 years. This combined with the economic downturn and resulting market uncertainty has yielded conservative hiring approaches by most reinsurers. Hours can also be longer at reinsurers as compared to primary carriers, though the times of heavier workload do tend to be cyclical and thus can be anticipated on an annual basis.

Switching Between Product Areas

As discussed previously, it can be difficult to switch product areas once you've begun your actuarial career. But it can be done, and it is easiest to do early in your career. The longer you wait to switch, the harder it will be to do so and the less likely employers will be willing to pay for your prior experience. For example, if a candidate earning $78,000 with 6 years of individual life experience wants to move to a defined benefit pension company, it is unlikely that the client is going to be willing to pay for those 6 years of life experience. The hiring manager would typically rather pay someone far more junior who has directly relevant work experience. In short, because the demand for junior level actuaries remains very strong, switching within your first 2 years of employment is not too difficult; 2-4 years of experience becomes more challenging but it can be done; and then starting with 4-6 years of experience, it becomes much more challenging. Over 6 years, you better have a good reason and be moving to a location in which it is hard to recruit actuaries and/or be willing to take a pay cut.

Recruiter Bias: There are many exceptions to these "guidelines above " and a knowledgeable recruiter can be of great assistance in several ways. First, experienced actuarial recruiters know which hiring managers and/or firms are more focused on exam passers (regardless of product experience). Recruiters can speak directly with those making hiring decisions to influence whose résumé is seen and who is actually interviewed. Second, hiring managers often trust the expertise and opinion of the recruiter (as their relationship may span many years and hired candidates). If this type of trust and confidence between the hiring manager and the recruiter exists, the life actuary (in the example above) just may get a telephone interview. At that point, however, it's up to that individual to "make the sale."

Please note that we define product areas broadly. Therefore, individuals moving from health insurance to health consulting or commercial lines to personal lines or moving from life insurance to life software development would not be considered to have changed product areas.

3

CAREER OPTIONS

Non Traditional Actuarial Avenues

Investment Work

Many actuaries express interest in "investment" or asset-side work. This familiar request has been asked of recruiters for decades with historically very few opportunities for actuaries to pursue. The first question I ask these individuals is what do you mean by "investments"? This is an important question because depending upon the area of "investments" or asset-side work, the likelihood of securing a position may be more difficult. There are 3 primary areas that I define as "investment":

1. Insurance Company Hedging Strategy Positions - Staying within the actuarial profession, working at an insurance company helping to design and implement hedging and derivative strategies for the company's asset management department.
2. Portfolio/Asset Management Positions - Leaving the actuarial profession, working as a portfolio manager at an asset management firm.
3. Securitization/Capital Markets Positions - Leaving the actuarial profession, working at a major investment bank (most likely in NYC) in the securitization / capital markets area.

Obtaining an Investment Position: The Basic Questions

The investment track is a popular area of interest for many actuaries in their careers. Hence, you need to be serious about it to have a chance to turn your goal into a reality. Here are three basic questions that you should ask yourself:

1. Are you willing to relocate?

Since investment opportunities for actuaries are still somewhat limited you must be geographically flexible. For many years, asset side work was primarily limited to a handful of jobs at investment banks in New York City and perhaps a few other opportunities in financial centers such as Boston or Chicago. Fortunately, the number of insurance companies hiring actuaries for hedging/derivatives strategy work, in particular, is increasing. So beyond the three cities listed above, you can add northern NJ, Philadelphia, Cedar Rapids, Minneapolis, and Baltimore. Of course we are leaving out a few locations. The point is, if you truly want an asset-side investment job, you are going to have to be geographically flexible. This point is especially valid if you are interested in portfolio management or securitization work. If you truly want asset-side work experience, outside of the traditional insurance company, you have to be willing to go where the jobs are located.

2. Are you willing to take a lateral move and/or interim steps to achieve a longer-term goal?

Another important consideration is whether or not you are willing to make the financial or career sacrifices necessary to obtain one of these positions. Asset side investment positions are difficult to obtain. Unlike the actuarial profession, supply exceeds demand when it comes to asset management positions. The field is much "sexier" and has lower barriers to entry, so there are considerably more qualified applicants for every open position. You will not get one simply by working as a pricing actuary at a midwest insurance company for 6 years. You must aggressively pursue the position by laying out a plan to achieve the goal. The best plan is typically to start early in your career by taking incremental steps toward asset-side work. Here are four recommended steps:

    a.   Pursue your Chartered Financial Analyst (CFA) designation, preferably very early in your actuarial career. As early as possible, you want to begin building your résumé for investment work. You cannot control your job rotations but you can begin and complete your CFA over a 3 year period. That being said, you are an actuary, and your actuarial background may be the easiest path to investment work. Therefore, I definitely suggest simultaneously pursuing your actuarial exams. Continuing with your actuarial exams is always helpful to your career as it gives you more impressive "credentials" and therefore greater employment flexibility. Unfortunately, pursuing your CFA has become somewhat more difficult because the actuarial profession has been dropped from the list of approved professions. CFA designations require a combination of work experience and passing 3 exams, each given only once per year. For more on the CFA designation please visit www.cfainstitute.com. To increase the likelihood of making a connection (and therefore not get declined at the few investment banks that actually hire actuaries), actuaries should wait to apply to these companies until after they complete their CFA. Other actuarial applicants will have an actuarial credential (ASA, FSA, ACAS, FCAS or E.A.) and their CFA. It will be a clear disadvantage to apply before you've earned your CFA. It's similar to applying for your first actuarial job without having passed an exam.

b. Pursue interim steps such as applying for asset-liability management (ALM) positions. ALM work will give you exposure to the work of the asset management teams. This is a helpful step toward doing the asset management work yourself. A small number of large insurance companies also offer actuaries work on the asset side of the balance sheet in areas focused on hedging and derivatives strategy. This is the most established and widespread opportunity for actuaries to get involved in "investment" work. The good news is that while opportunities in this area remain small, they are growing as more insurance companies implement advanced hedging and derivatives strategies to manage their reserve assets. If you are a high performing employee, watch for internal openings and inquire about them if they become available. At Pinnacle Group, we frequently work on positions of this nature.

c. An actuary's easiest entry point to this industry can sometimes be through their expertise in insurance. A handful of investment banks and specialty asset management groups specialize in asset management for the insurance industry or for large pension plans (Taft-Hartley plans, in particular). Focusing your job search efforts on these niche investment management firms helps you leverage your distinguishing (actuarial) asset. To prepare for these types of positions, it would be very helpful to have earned your FSA or

FCAS as well as your CFA combined with 5+ years of actuarial modeling experience, perhaps on both the asset and liability side of the balance sheet.

When applying for asset/portfolio management positions outside of this focus on insurance, your résumé becomes far less attractive relative to the pool of other qualified candidates. Outside the insurance industry, you are competing with MBAs with CFAs who often already have many years of asset/portfolio management experience. In addition, many of these MBAs have graduate degrees from the top MBA programs in the country. Due to the huge number of applicants for these positions, investment banks use the graduate school you attended as a pre-screening tool. If you didn't go to a top 10 or top 15 business school, the odds of your résumé being reviewed at all drop significantly. To give an example, if you are an actuary who attended GA State or UCONN (which have great actuarial science programs) for your B.A. in Actuarial Science and then attended Boston University or Temple University for your MBA (which have modest reputations for graduate business degrees) it is likely your entry into the hyper-selective investment (non-insurance related) world will be more difficult. Not impossible, but more difficult for sure. Right or wrong, it is the Ivy League schools, plus the Stanfords, the Univ. of Chicagos that jump off the résumé page and that is what investment banks are typically seeking.

d. Get your foot in the door. Gaining entry into the actuarial profession where demand far outweighs supply is much easier than gaining entry into the asset management industry where the reverse is the case. For this reason, actuaries must change their way of thinking about career progression. To gain entry into this much more competitive field, they have to be prepared to accept a step in the right direction and not worry if, in the short-term, it is a step up in responsibility or compensation. If you have an opportunity to work for a major investment bank or asset management firm, for example, take it. Don't quibble that you were earning $60,000 in Des Moines and they are only paying you $62,000 to work in New York City. Don't worry that they don't have a student program or that they don't offer a relocation package to help you move. Sooner than you may know, compensation will take care of itself and you'll likely be very pleased with both the type of work and the long-term compensation. I would argue that if you are offered a job at Goldman Sachs, stapling papers together, take it. Don't quibble about salary, don't worry that it's not exactly what you were looking for. Take it. It is your entry point. From there, the sky is the limit. If you are good, you'll start off "stapling papers" and end up managing portfolios. Similarly, if you are lucky enough to be offered a position managing asset portfolios for a smaller asset management company in Hartford, CT, take it. This is your entry point. From there, you can absolutely make your way to other "sexier" companies if you are talented and that is your desire. You need a start, and in this very competitive industry, a start is very difficult to get. Don't let shortsighted thinking or your ego keep you from getting into the game.

3.   *Are you willing to accept significantly less job security?*

Working as a traditional actuary has one major advantage over nearly every other profession and that is job security. Even in today's weaker employment marketplace, Pinnacle Group estimates that 99% of all actuaries and actuarial students are either employed or re-employed within six months of losing their position. And frankly, actuaries are rarely laid off even during turbulent economic times. Wall Streeters, by comparison, are not as fortunate. Even in the midst of a slow economic recovery, Wall Street eliminated close to 300,000 jobs during 2011 and 2012 (*Bloomberg Business Week*, 12/5/2012.) In the good years, Wall Street is still a "what have you done for me lately business" with plenty of aggressive and eager applicants waiting to fill your shoes should you be let go. In the investment industry, performance is easily measured and management typically moves swiftly to promptly address "underperformance" by its staff. In many cases, this creates a competitive, cut throat and performance driven culture that will differ vastly from that of an insurance carrier. If considering a change to a bank or investment advisor, investigate the corporate culture of the firm and think seriously about if such a culture is right for you in your career.

Enterprise Risk Management / CERA

The Society of Actuaries (SOA) is promoting enterprise risk management (ERM) as one of the most effective tools for managing the broad risks insurers and other institutions face. In fact, in 2007 the SOA created a new designation, the Chartered Enterprise Risk Analyst (CERA), to support this effort. The idea behind the CERA designation is to promote the notion that actuaries can do more in the risk management arena than simply pricing and reserving for insurance companies. However, as it currently stands, the CERA designation is essentially an "add on" to the current professional education that any pre-ASA would gain in pursuit of the Associate (ASA) designation. This may change over time. But today, as a recruiter, I view the CERA designation as mostly a "marketing effort" by the SOA. As noted above, the SOA is attempting to say to a much wider audience of employers, "Hey, actuaries can do more than pricing and reserving!" And of course, they are absolutely right. An actuary's keen analytical skills can be used in a variety of ways within an organization, including risk management applications outside the insurance industry. Unfortunately, the broader employment marketplace is simply not demanding those skills from actuaries at this time. As discussed previously, there is a shortage of experienced actuaries, including those needed to do traditional pricing and reserving work. Our insurance clients want those jobs filled first. As a result, we have only had a few insurance clients ever request candidates with the CERA designation. It appears certain that growth in the employment of actuaries in ERM roles outside of the insurance industry will be slow and modest. Within the insurance industry, however, we are seeing robust demand for actuaries to fill ERM roles.

Careers Combining Actuarial with IT

Another career path for actuaries is in the area of software development, actuarial systems or data warehousing. These opportunities are fairly abundant and growing modestly. It is a great choice for actuaries with a strong interest in this type of work and for those who do not wish to necessarily continue with actuarial exams. Most of these positions are filled by actuarial students who have stopped pursuing Fellowship.

Software Development Firms

There are many actuarial software development firms located around the country. Most are relatively small companies but there are also opportunities within the software development divisions of large consulting firms such as Towers Watson and Milliman. The work at the software development firms normally takes one of two paths; programming/software development or client sales, implementation and support. The software development side is programming focused. Technical skills are the most important hiring criteria for these types of positions. The "client side" helps market and sell the software, implement the product at the client site and then provides post-sale training and ongoing support. This role typically requires some travel, frequent client interaction and strong communication skills.

Insurance Companies

Many insurance companies are expanding their staff in the areas of actuarial, and administrative systems and data warehousing. There are a number of reasons for this, but the three most important are regulation, improved efficiency, and pricing. Insurance companies are highly regulated and having the right technology and systems can help the company better prepare data for regulatory review. Better data can lead to greatly improved administrative efficiencies as well. Finally, better data, analyzed properly, can dramatically improve the actuarial staff's ability to manage risk and price products more appropriately. To have a member of the systems or warehousing team with experience in actuarial pricing, reserving, filing, reporting, etc. can be tremendously helpful. The actuarial department often depends heavily on data generated by these teams. The better the data, the easier and better the job is completed.

Implications

It is important to note that leaving the traditional actuarial path and pursuing a career on the "systems" side is not without implications. Generally speaking, "systems" positions pay less than the traditional actuarial career path. Moving to "systems" will also signal to future employers that this is your area of interest and will likely limit you ability to return back to the traditional actuarial path. Fortunately, if you do need to change employers, these types of positions are generally available throughout the country.

Other Areas

I'll be adding to this section. If you have any suggestions, please email me at tom@pinnaclejobs.com

Consulting V. Insurance

Overview

Consulting versus insurance is a topic that is discussed often and at great length by many actuaries (and recruiters). As might be expected, there is no simple answer to which career path might be best for you. There are many variables that must be considered that are directly related to each company, office location and individual. In most instances, the single most important variable is neither "consulting" nor "insurance". It's your boss and your boss' boss. Regardless if it is an insurance company or a consulting office environment, your direct supervisor and often your supervisor's boss, sets the tone for the office. They create and mold the overall atmosphere, and will set expectations for work hours, work-life balance, study time and the level of professionalism. Of course, they also largely determine such critical factors as compensation and job responsibilities including promotions, project leads, and other assignments.

The stereotype of the actuarial consultant working 80 hours per week while receiving very limited study time and the insurance actuary working half as much with a full allocation of study hours is inaccurate. It is a generalization with some basis in fact, but there are tens of thousands of actuarial jobs in consulting and insurance and are all influenced by different factors. Therefore, when interviewing for a new position, it is very important that you try to ascertain the type of office culture your supervisor and his/her boss promote among the relevant staff.

That being said, I will endeavor to outline the key considerations and most notable differences between consulting and insurance to consider when contemplating your career decision. In doing so, I will necessarily make some generalizations as a way to heighten your awareness to the issues. I strongly recommend however, that you put aside any preconceived notions when exploring your employment options and investigate each opportunity on its own merits.

Key Considerations

Do you want to work with clients?

The most important question about whether or not you should be a consultant or at least explore working at a consulting firm is assessing whether or not you might like working directly with external clients. In addition, you should consider if you'd prefer to work in a smaller office environment (consulting) or a much larger one (insurance). Consulting offices are smaller and therefore you are likely to gain exposure to clients relatively quickly as your experience builds. As an actuary at an insurance company, your "clients" are individuals within your organization, actuaries at the state insurance department, reinsurance actuaries or perhaps outside vendors.

As a recruiter, I have found that most actuaries feel that consulting either intrinsically appeals to them or it does not. If it appeals to you, or if you are not sure, I recommend exploring consulting as an option. Think about what your "gut" tells you about working with clients and the nature of consulting work. If you feel you may enjoy it, then investigate it. Each firm and each office within each firm is different and you may find an exciting opportunity awaits you.

Is there a quality of life trade off with consulting?

The answer to the above questions is an unequivocal "sometimes". As a consultant, you may have less time at home. Often this may be due to greater travel requirements rather than longer work hours. This is especially true as you increase your level of client responsibility. That being said, there are some consulting positions (precious few) that require little or no travel. Regardless of the job, if you have to travel for work and you don't enjoy it, the days become that much longer.

Most of the major consulting firms have taken steps to attract and retain talented employees, in particular more women and minorities. Turnover is costly to all companies and consulting firms have attempted to address these issues with flexible work schedules and more regular total work hours. But at the end of the day, your boss and the client determines if you make it home for dinner that night. Of course, deadlines must be met at an insurance company as well. Therefore, as noted above, much of the work-hours difference between consulting and insurance will fall to your boss, the amount of travel that you undertake and the time of year (within the business cycle.)

Please keep in mind that most consulting position descriptions, whether posted on the web or provided by a recruiter, are generic job postings that only provide a broad overview of the work that you might expect in the role. They will not have any true job-specific information regarding the office specialty areas, their primary client focus, the hours worked, the amount of study time given or the amount of travel. For example, the position descriptions will nearly always state, "travel 0-20%". This is just boilerplate language along with many other bullets on the job description. This is why I stated above that you must determine in advance if you think you'd like to explore consulting because it intrinsically appeals to you. Without speaking directly to one of the hiring managers, you will not get a true sense of what it means to be an actuarial consultant within that particular office with that particular firm. Just as within the insurance company universe, job responsibilities and work hours can vary widely from office to office, and engagement to engagement, even within the same firm. It is up to you to investigate, to the best of your ability, the factors that are most important to you before making a job change.

Will I get my study time?

This is always an important question to consider. Early in your career, a great deal of time and energy is focused on balancing the need to effectively manage your workload at the office with the time required to pass the actuarial exams. Most individuals at this level want to know if the company has a good "student program". Fortunately almost all employers of actuaries have competitive student programs that pay for examination fees, required textbooks and other study aids and provide paid time off to study for each exam. If your current employer does not offer these benefits, you may want to consider changing jobs.

Insurance companies are usually more likely to provide greater flexibility than consulting firms regarding scheduling time off for exam preparation and may be somewhat more likely to provide the full amount of exam study hours as outlined in their student programs. Please note, however, that both insurance and consulting positions focused on seasonal accounting/audit support functions will be far less likely to allow for time off during the peak busy seasons. In these types of positions, preparing for Spring exams can often prove more difficult than preparing for Fall exams. You may also find that larger insurance companies and larger consulting practices are better able to provide more flexible exam study time due to their larger staffs. Larger staffs often, but not always, allow for an improved ability to shift work around during the days leading up to an exam.

Passing exams at a reasonable pace is quite important to the careers of most actuaries. When you are considering employment in consulting, you must recognize that it is a "client comes first environment". This means that scheduled time off for exam preparation is sometimes more difficult in consulting environments. It is also important to recognize that differences in staffing levels, client activity and the management style of the practice leader all contribute to variations in available study time. Study time varies between different firms, different offices of the same firm, and even within different consulting practices (e.g., life, pension, P&C) in the same office of the same firm.

As a recruiting firm, Pinnacle Group would love to provide you a list of where you can get plenty of study time and where you do not but it changes with some frequency for the reasons discussed previously. The best advice that we can give you is the following: during the "in-office" interview process, ask appropriate individuals about student program. Specifically, inquire regarding how successful that office/practice has been in providing their current actuarial students with the stated study time outlined in their program documents. You may also want to ask about the exam pass rates of other actuarial students currently in that office/practice. Please note, however, that we strongly suggest that these inquiries only be made at the "office level", during an in-person interview or when speaking with an actuary at the specific office for which you are being considered. You will likely get far more accurate information at this stage of the interview process. When conducting a telephone interview with Human Resources staff, the individual is typically located outside of the city for which you are interviewing and he or she will not possess enough office-specific information to answer these questions. These questions are best left for current actuarial students who work at the firm or the office practice leader.

Overall, you will likely get somewhat less study time at consulting firms as compared to insurance opportunities. It is our view that consulting firms recognize this fact and attempt to hire actuarial students who not only have a strong interest and aptitude for client work but who may also require less study time to pass exams. For this reason, it is far less likely that consulting firms will consider you for employment if you are having difficulty passing exams. Consulting firms want to you to pass exams. In fact, it is quite important to them that you do pass. As a consultant, you are hired to be an expert. Achieving fellowship is typically very important to your credibility as a Lead Consultant/Principal. And while consulting firms can always hire externally at the FSA or FCAS level, as with most companies, they would prefer to hire actuarial students and groom them to take on positions of greater responsibility in the future.

Compensation

Compensation is addressed more fully in another section of the book but I'll address the topic here, specifically as it relates to consulting versus insurance.

For entry-level hires, compensation is likely to be slightly better at a consulting firm. This is primarily due to large consulting firms competing for the best actuarial talent (or perceived potential talent). Over time, this has modestly boosted the pay for entry-level actuarial students entering consulting. But many large insurance companies also compete for this "select talent pool" and so you may find a handful of insurance companies offering very similar or even higher pay. Either way, your pay will be competitive. Most actuarial students start their careers with a base salary of $45,000 to $55,000 with some minor variations due to location (cost of living) and the number of exams passed. Raises or bonuses for passing exams as well as annual performance bonuses are nearly always offered in addition to base salary.

As you gain expertise and advance in your career, compensation between insurance and consulting will become less equal. On average, consulting actuaries will earn more than their peers at insurance companies. Though there is always the argument that on an hourly basis, insurance company professionals earn more. Generally speaking, that argument is valid. However, when it comes to compensation, much will depend upon your individual performance. With each year of experience, the egalitarian nature of those early "student program" days fade. Over time, it is no secret who the best performers are and they will be paid accordingly. This is true regardless of where you work.

At what point in my career should I consider a change to consulting if I am interested?

It is common for Pre-Associate, ASAs and ACAS actuarial students to say, "I'd like to switch to consulting after getting my Fellowship." Often unstated is: "I want to get my exams out of the way before trying consulting." This approach has merits but perhaps more pitfalls than most recognize.

First, let's examine the opportunity for "junior level" actuarial consultants. Beginning your actuarial career in consulting or switching to it from an insurance company early in your career is easier than at the Fellow level. At the Fellow level, consulting firms are primarily seeking to hire candidates with prior consulting experience. If you don't have prior consulting experience, it can be difficult to get it once you become an FSA or FCAS. Therefore, gaining two years or more of consulting experience as an actuarial student can be very helpful to you later in your career.

When consulting firms seek to hire externally, most strongly prefer to hire Fellows with prior consulting experience (the more, the better). The reason for this is simple. If they are going to pay you six figures, they want you to be able to make an immediate impact with client leadership and/or client development. Fellows and other senior actuaries coming from an insurance background often cannot "hit the ground running". In consulting circles, it is often believed that these individuals have difficulty quickly transitioning to the diversity and pace of the consulting environment. Now, individuals with insurance backgrounds are hired by consulting firms at all levels. However, the more senior you become, the more challenging it becomes to be hired by a consulting firm. You become a high-risk hire. To put it into mathematical terms: Big salary + Zero Consulting Experience = Low Probability of Consulting Hire.

It is worth noting here that the reverse can also happen. Senior consultants are paid quite well and have excellent experience with a broad array of products. They have often developed highly sought after experience in a particular area. However, they frequently lack significant management experience. Senior Consultants earning in excess of $170,000 are likely pursuing VP level positions or above. These positions will often manage staff sizes of 10+ individuals. Consultants with limited management experience, regardless of their product or functional expertise, will be at a disadvantage when interviewing for these senior management posts because of concerns regarding their people management experience and skills. To put it into mathematical terms: Big Consulting Salary + Zero Management Experience = Low Probability of Senior Management Hire.

If an actuarial student is interested in consulting, we recommend they make the switch before obtaining their FSA or FCAS. This advice is contrary to what many actuarial students would prefer to do. Most actuarial students would prefer to make the change after they have completed exams. New fellows are still in demand by consulting firms, especially if you have the right personality and fast exam progress, but you will undoubtedly have greater pressure on you to produce value sooner. However, near fellows with slightly lower compensation (than new fellows), have the benefit of somewhat lower immediate expectations. ASAs and ACASs are generally given less responsibility than Fellows and thus may have more time to get acclimated to the consulting world. They can begin to develop their consulting skills with less pressure to make an immediate impact related to client leadership and development. And while you may have to finish one of more exams, as stated above, consulting firms have an interest in helping you do so.

A second consideration is that working at a consulting firm can offer actuarial students a wider range of work, thereby broadening skills and increasing your options for next steps in your career. This is particularly true outside of the benefits consulting area. Consulting firms that focus on life & annuity, P&C and health insurance (note: I'm excluding health and retirement benefits consultants from this discussion) will typically have their junior actuarial staff working on a wide variety of projects, increasing your exposure to many different products and functional skills. Actuarial students at insurance companies typically rotate to different areas. Both backgrounds can be appealing to future employers for different reasons.

Differences Between Consulting and Insurance Careers

Please keep in mind that given the expected length of your career, you may have the opportunity to work at both insurance and consulting firms. Movement between the two areas is common. Deciding if and when to pursue consulting or insurance work will be an individual decision. It will depend significantly on your career interests as well as the stage of your career. For this reason, we thought it helpful to divide the discussion into 3 sections, early- mid- and late-career.

Early-Career (the first five years)

Responsibilities at insurance companies are typically well defined. Your area of responsibility has structure and periodic deliverables. This structure allows for the development of deeper expertise within a particular area. The longer you work in that particular area the more expertise you develop with group health pricing, commercial auto reserving, term life valuation, etc. It also allows for incremental and consistent steps toward common markers for professional development such as management experience and profit and loss responsibilities. As you gain experience, prove your talents and move up in the organization, you have the opportunity to assume greater responsibility.

These are, however, still the early years of your career. Given the hierarchy at most insurance companies, these years will typically be focused on more technical, data intensive responsibilities such as experience studies or rate filing. The data intensive responsibilities may require Excel® macro or programming skills.

Larger insurance companies have more products, more functional areas, and more hierarchy than smaller firms. Therefore, at a larger company you will be more focused within a particular area. The good news however, is that many larger insurance companies offer rotational student programs. These rotational programs are typically organized by a member of the Actuarial or Human Resources staff and help with your career development by diversifying your experience. Job rotations are typically 18-24 months in length. For example, at a life insurance company you might have a first rotation in life pricing, a second rotation in annuity valuation and a third rotation in corporate planning. This is terrific work experience and with each rotation, you'll likely move up the hierarchy, taking on greater responsibility. You'll also have opportunity to assess your interest level in different functional/product areas of the industry before settling into a specialty.

Smaller insurance companies do not often have formal rotational programs. This doesn't mean that you won't be able to switch jobs internally and gain new experiences. At smaller insurance companies, by their nature, you will almost always have broader responsibilities. For example, you may be involved in pricing across the company's life and annuity lines or you may handle pricing, reserving/valuation and forecasting for a particular product line. Finally, you may find that you gain earlier exposure to senior management at a smaller insurance company.

Junior level actuaries at consulting firms are also typically responsible for technical, data intensive work. The difference is that in the consulting arena, the work is determined by the needs of the various clients. Client projects are typically directed by a Senior Consultant. You'll be assigned to assist with various projects for different Senior Consultants. This creates a less structured work environment that necessitates project-driven work for multiple clients simultaneously. The benefit of consulting is that you will have the opportunity to work on a wide range of projects for various clients spanning pricing, reserving/valuation, filing, statement reporting, etc. This can be exciting work and may lead to broader experience more quickly. This, however, depends a great deal upon the individual circumstances of what type of consulting you are doing, the firm you work for and where you are working. For example, defined benefit (DB) pension consulting is largely a self-contained industry practice area. The skills that you are developing as a DB consultant are excellent but they are mostly applicable only at a DB consulting firm. Conversely, a life consultant will develop skills that will be in demand at both life insurance companies and other life consulting firms. So it is possible that you may obtain "better experience faster" at a life consulting firm versus an insurance company. "Better" is always a relative term, of course, and I use it here referring to your marketability as a candidate for employment.

Mid-career (Years 6-14)

It is during this period of time in the actuarial profession (and many other professions) when separation due to individual performance begins to really take hold. Stronger achievers will begin to noticeably separate from their peers due to better on-the-job performance, faster exam progress or both. It is also during this period when your actuarial product specialization begins to cement. By this I mean, if you've been a Group Health actuary for the past 6 years, you are unlikely to ever leave health insurance during your career. You might dabble in individual health (Medicare Supplement for example) or group non-medical products such as Group Life or Disability but for the most part, actuaries are "fixed" into their respective products areas by their sixth year of employment.

Due to this separation, it becomes harder to make broad generalizations though I will try for the purposes of this book. For example, at this point in your career at an insurance company, you may have the opportunity for your first meaningful supervisory or management experience. This is always beneficial to a career. Managing people is not always easy or fun but developing these skills will help prepare you for bigger opportunities later in your career. These management skills will also be in demand by both insurance and consulting firms. Most consultants do not manage large staffs but when hiring for their offices, they will often seek individuals with strong "people" skills and demonstrated career progression.

At a consulting firm, you may have the opportunity to lead client engagements and/or become involved in client development. Both indicate career progression and are therefore always helpful to your career prospects. At this point, you have also likely begun to develop a strong expertise in a particular product area. Having worked on different client projects over the years will give you better perspective on the marketplace for your specialty area than you may have received by working at one or two insurance companies. You may also begin to appreciate the reduced bureaucracy found at most consulting firms.

Late Career (Years 15+)

After 15 years in the industry you may find that your career has started to plateau. Earlier in their careers most actuaries who attain Fellowship find that as they progress through their exams, they are bestowed with frequent increases in both responsibility and pay. Some of this advancement is institutionalized within the organizations based upon exam achievements. In many ways, this early career progression is easier than what lies ahead. It is practically expected that an FSA or FCAS will be promoted into a Director/ AVP or Senior Consultant level position. It is far more difficult to continue to move up into VP, SVP or Principal level positions, however. Why is this so? Well for starters, there are fewer of these positions available. Therefore, these individuals must show skills beyond just impressive technical actuarial analyses. Most notably these skills include:

- Superior people/management skills
- General business and insurance industry savvy
- Very strong work ethic
- Strong professional network (within and outside of current employer)
- High level of commitment to advancing the goals of the firm

Of particular note are the first two: superior people/management skills and general business savvy. To be successful at the highest levels, though, you need all five. It is my view that people/management skills are learned. Some individuals learn them (or at least many critical aspects of them) at an early age, before they enter the work force. Many learn them "on the job" starting with modest supervisory roles overseeing 1-2 people. But regardless of when we learn them, it is important to recognize the simple fact that we can all be better, more effective managers. The actuaries who consciously and proactively develop those skills will be the ones who are most likely offered VP or Senior Management level roles. If your company offers workshops on developing your managerial skills, take them. You will benefit, your company will benefit, and your future staff will benefit. This statement is true regardless of whether you are at an insurance company or consulting firm.

Recommended Books for Managers

- *The 7 Habits of Highly Effective People,* Stephen R. Covey
- *Leadership and Self-Deception,* Arbinger Institute
- *The One Minute Manager,* Kenneth H. Blanchard
- *The 21 Irrefutable Laws of Leadership,* John C. Maxwell
- *The Five Dysfunctions of a Team,* Patrick Lencioni
- *First Break All the Rules,* Marcus Buckingham
- *The Leadership Challenge,* Jim Kouzes
- *The First 90 Days,* Michael Watkins
- *How to Win Friends and Influence People,* Dale Carnegie
- *Good to Great,* Jim Collins
- *It's Your Ship,* Michael Abrashoff

A second reason why actuaries plateau is that they do not develop skill sets outside of technical actuarial work. This can be more difficult to overcome because your job description may not lend itself to you developing other needed skills and competencies. As you evolve in your career it's important to keep a current understanding of industry trends, product distribution (spend some time with those pesky sales and marketing people!), enterprise risk and, of course, to hone your management skills. I have referred a few times already to communication skills and I'll repeat it again here. Your ability to communicate effectively up, down and across an organization (or to clients if you are a consultant) will, without question, differentiate you as you become more seasoned in your career. What can you do if your current role does not provide sufficient opportunity to develop the above? Join a society committee, publish a paper, attend conferences, seek out training and leadership development opportunities within the company you work for. The sooner you get started down this path of development, the earlier it will make a positive impact on your career and in your paycheck.

4

CONDUCTING A JOB SEARCH

Considerations Before Beginning a Job Search

Let's admit it: looking for a new job is not fun. It can be quite stressful. There are many factors outside of your control and timelines for the process can stretch out for what seems like an eternity. "Hurry up and wait" is often an apt description of the process. In practice, nearly all candidates can improve the search process more to their liking, as I will outline in this section. Before we get to that topic however, you must first determine why you want to change jobs. For most of you, the answer to this question will be obvious and your reason(s) sound, but it does warrant a brief review.

The most important step before beginning a search is determining why you want to leave your current role and/or what professional and personal priorities you would like to pursue. It is paramount that you "take inventory" of why you want to change jobs and what types of opportunities you believe may be of interest professionally.

The most common reasons for a voluntary job change include:

- Balance & Support—Improved work/life balance (including geographic moves to be near family/support)
- Advancement—New skill development and challenges; greater responsibility
- Compensation—More is always better than less! (closely associated with "advancement")
- Environment—Excessive workload, lack of support, company financial difficulties
- Personal Frustration—Lack of personal enjoyment; insufficient challenge or meaning in the job

All of the above reasons are valid rationale for a job change, and of course there are other perfectly good reasons to begin a job search. Or there could be multiple reasons. Just be careful how you phrase "Show me the money!" during an interview. Generally speaking, actuaries are not NFL superstars and must approach negotiations with a bit more tact.

Another important consideration is communicating your thoughts and plans with loved ones who will be affected by the change in job. Speak honestly with them. Their input will undoubtedly be important to you and may influence your search goals. Not only will they help you sort out the why's, where's and how's of a job change, but they need to "buy-in" to the entire search effort. You would be surprised how often a spouse or significant other is only partially aware of the seriousness of a full-blown job search by their partner. Perhaps the spouse is simply trying to bury their head in the sand and not confront the pending change? Whatever, the reason, it can lead to considerable shock when the decision to accept an employment offer presents itself. In these situations, the reaction from the loved one is frequently, "No, I'm not ready." They will feel pressured and rushed. This may be true regardless of how long you have been looking for a new position, especially if you haven't communicated the seriousness of your job search fully.

Beginning Your Search: Where the Rubber Meets the Road

Step 1: Select Your References

This may surprise you, but I recommend you start your job search with your references. For most people, reference checks are commonly one of the final steps in the job search process. Prospective employers normally complete reference checks right before a formal offer of employment is extended. So why start there? The reason is that a lot of hard work and time goes into a job search. You certainly don't want to go through all the trouble of a job search just to find out that you cannot locate your former bosses or to find that company policy will not allow them to serve as a reference for you. Worse yet, you could find out that they are unlikely to provide a positive reference. For these reasons, the best time to begin thinking about and contacting your references is early in your search, not at the last minute. Begin with these 3 tasks:

1. Locate and speak directly with the potential references. Email is great for many things but please pick up the phone. You'll be able to communicate much more effectively through a conversation.
2. Make sure that they can provide a <u>positive</u> reference. Emphasize that you want to be sure that they are comfortable providing a positive reference. If they cannot assure you of that, then thank them for their time and find another reference.
3. Let each reference know that in the weeks or months ahead, you'll be back in contact with them with the specifics of who will be calling from which company.

During your job search, it is important to keep in periodic contact with your references. If you know that an offer is likely going to be made and that they will be calling your references, call your references first. Make sure they are aware of who will be calling from what company and just as important, make sure to communicate your keen interest in the position. Basically, you should let each reference know, "Hey, I really want this job. Please provide the best reference you can."

Step 2: Determine if There Are Any Special Search Circumstances

Special search circumstances are anything that may make your search more difficult. Examples of special search circumstances include:

- Returning to work force after an absence
- Employment visa related issues (NAFTA, F1, H1-B)
- Recently laid off / currently unemployed
- Seeking part-time or telecommute options
- Changing careers to actuarial from another profession
- Seeking "non-traditional" and/or non-actuarial work (data warehousing, capital markets, asset management, programming)
- Changing product specialty (e.g., from life to P&C)
- No longer pursuing actuarial exams (below Fellow level)
- Seeking international positions
- Need to also relocate a spouse/partner to the same location
- Entry-level

If you match any of the criteria above, your search may take longer. There will be fewer companies interested in considering you for their openings, and those that are interested may not match your goals. But all is not lost and we will discuss career conundrums in the pages ahead.

Step 3: Put Together a Strong Résumé

Your résumé is your marketing document. The content, organization, and layout of your résumé is paramount to your search effort. This is true at every step of your career but it becomes even more important as you advance in your profession. I've included examples of strong résumés in the Appendix. The examples shown follow the "dos and don'ts" listed below.

DO include on your résumé:

- Achievements/Impact Made- Quantify where possible
- Company or Professional Awards
- Dates of employment
- Specific product areas you were responsible for
- Citizenship/Employment status (if you believe it may be uncertain)
- Specific Job Responsibilities Held
- Number of People Managed / Supervised
- Current Contact Info (don't include your work number)
- SOA/CAS/EA Exams passed (if relevant)

It is important that your two most recent positions contain the greatest amount of detail. Most interviewers are going to focus their attention and questions on what you have done in the past five years, with secondary interest on work experience and achievements in years prior to the most recent role. A good rule of thumb is at least one line of content for every year that you worked at a company with a three line minimum. If you can't fill out at least 3 lines worth of responsibilities then you were/are probably overpaid!

Optional to Include:

- Summary of career (for those who have worked 10+ years, should be no more than 3 well worded sentences)
- Scores on exams (9s and 10s are typically best to list)
- GPA (only if you had a minimum of 3.5 or higher)
- Listing of published articles, reports (definitely include if they are directly related to actuarial or other work related topics)
- Company name changes (e.g., "Aviva (Formerly AmerUs)")
- Company description (only if the company is not well known or if the work experience at this company is outside the fields of insurance or actuarial)

- Hobbies (If you feel you must include hobbies, stay conservative with those you do list. In most cases, listing hobbies won't materially enhance your résumé, but they can detract from it if not chosen wisely.)

Do NOT include:

- Career Objectives
- High School information
- Lots of junior level info (If you are a senior level candidate)
- Too much personal information
- Graphics
- Website links
- Photos
- References
- The statement, "References available upon request"

A brief word about why I suggest not including a career objective on your résumé. The first reason is that too often, people write terrible objectives. I describe them as terrible because either they say very little of importance, and therefore are somewhat bland and meaningless; or worse, they are too specific, and thereby communicate the wrong things to hiring managers. Of the two problem types of objectives, the bland objective is the least harmful to your employment chances. It's like wearing a bad suit to an interview; you can overcome it, but the rest of your interview had better go well! Unfortunately, many people submit résumés with objectives that are too specific and/or don't match the open position. This happens frequently and when it does, I'm sure you can guess the result. The hiring personnel stops reading and puts your résumé in the "no" pile.

To be effective, objectives have to be exceptionally well written. They must outline your short and long-term professional objectives, highlight how you will leverage your existing experience to add value to the goals of the organizations and do so in a manner that demonstrates positive employment traits (such as leadership, motivation, interpersonal/team skills, etc). Most people fall well short of a strong, well-written career objective that makes a positive impact on their résumé.

It is important to remember that your career objective and your entire résumé should be reviewed (better yet, scrutinized) before submitting it to each and every company. If you insist on including a well-written objective, tweaking it to fit the open position can be a good approach. Unfortunately, it's difficult to keep track of what résumé version you uploaded to what company website or sent to which recruiting firm. Staying organized in this manner may sound easy, but it's difficult in practice. When you show up for the on-site interview, you want the résumé in your hand to perfectly match the résumé sitting in front of the hiring personnel. Differing versions can create "red flags" or concern about your true interest in the current opening.

Finally, there is the issue of company application tracking software and the fact that your résumé may stay on file for months or even years. After initially applying for one position, you may have an interest in other positions at the company. Will the company review your résumé in several months for a new opening? If your career objective does not match the new job responsibilities, you may be passed over again, even though you would have been interested and qualified for position.

My advice on career objectives is to leave them off. Let your experience dictate how the hiring manager views your fit for the position.

Tips For a Standout Résumé

- Pay attention to style and format. A strong résumé is visually appealing and easy to read. This is most easily accomplished by using a common text such as Times New Roman, a font size of 11 or 12 point (10 point minimum), and by avoiding the use of logos, designs, special characters or pictures.
- Use **bold**, CAPITALIZATION, *italics* and underlining in a consistent manner. But beware of too much formatting which can yield a document that is too busy to the eye.
- Your experience should be in chronological order, from the most recent back to the oldest.
- Do not put your résumé in the first person. (ex: "I have been pricing annuities . . .")
- Use meaningful action—oriented verbs: manage, analyze, etc.

- Include all institutions of higher education you have attended, including your GPA if you feel comfortable, and it is high (over 3.5/4.0)
- Note your Society of Actuaries designation(s), if any, and exam credit total. For Pre-Associates, it is often helpful to cite those exams you have completed.
- The 1 Page Rule? Your résumé can be more than one page, especially as you advance in your career. It is best if you can keep it to two pages. And a two page résumé is always better than squeezing your résumé onto one page with narrow margins and small fonts. A third page should only be used if you are particularly accomplished and/ or have 15+ years of work experience. Four pages are too many. If you have a fourth page listing articles published, for example, offer it as a separate document.
- If you've held multiple, distinct positions with the same company, do separate out each position by job title and responsibilities. Be sure to include the months or years in each position.
- If you've expanded your responsibilities within the same job area and received a promotion(s), you can exclude earlier titles. If you've been with the company for 4+ years, and you want to show career progression, however, it might be a good idea to list each promotion as follows:

ABC Life Insurance Company
Vice President—Actuarial Pricing (January 2011-Present)
Assistant Vice President—Actuarial Pricing (January 2008-December 2010)

- After 3 years of work experience, your education should typically be at the end of your résumé. If you graduated from Ivy League caliber schools, perhaps you can keep it there a bit longer but most actuaries have not attended Harvard or M.I.T.
- Spellcheck! Proofread! Spellcheck again! (Ask a friend to do the same.)

Due to the nature of our jobs, all Pinnacle Group recruiters are résumé experts by default! Seek our advice and suggestions- we are happy to help you with your résumé.

Résumé & Career Conundrums

Résumés reflect your career. Life events or other factors result in situations that might reflect negatively if not addressed properly on your résumé and/or during the interview process. For now, I'll focus on the following issues and how they should be handled on your résumé.

- Breaks in employment: Be accurate with your dates. The tendency is to want to cover up breaks in your employment. It will hurt more if it is later discovered that you fudged the dates. Most companies conduct background checks and will rescind an offer if inaccuracies are found.

- Jobs held only a short period: Let me start by recommending that you try your best to work at each company for a minimum of two years! With that said, the best reason for leaving a job after only a short period of time is that you were recruited to work for a former manager or there was a big organizational change that resulted in the loss of employment or the threat of loss of employment. If you are working with a recruiter, getting this information to the hiring personnel should be fairly easy. If you are applying on your own, I might suggest addressing it very briefly in your cover letter.

- You are very experienced: Candidates with more than 20 years of experience are often concerned about age discrimination in the market and approach us about how best to navigate this threat with their résumés. While it may be tempting to leave off past positions and dates of college graduation, we encourage candidates to present themselves directly and in a straightforward manner. Otherwise you risk an internal recruiter or hiring manager feeling like they've been lied to or duped when you sit down in front of them and you are older then your résumé inferred you would be. It's not the right foot to start off an interview on, and won't create a feeling of trust in you from the employer. Make sure you practice for the interview and are able to demonstrate how your wealth of experience will add value to the position in question.

- Involuntary Dismissals: An involuntary dismissal is one of the hardest "conundrums" to address successfully. Once it's known that you were let go involuntarily, it is hard to overcome, unless it was related to a company-wide layoff. And even that can be challenging. That being said, most actuaries are very conscientious, hard working and professional. There may be very good reasons that it simply didn't work out. Not every person is a match with every manager or every job. You likely (hopefully) learned a great deal from the experience, turning a job negative into a career positive for many years to come. The best way around this résumé problem is through properly selecting and vetting your references. You need to make 100% sure that each reference you select can provide a positive reference. As discussed earlier in this section, this is your most important first step. It is also critical that you practice how you will discuss the issue of your involuntary dismissal in an interview, as you can be assured questions will arise.

Step 4: Review Social Media / Personal Items

Social media can be your friend and your foe in a job search. Let's start with the positive first. LinkedIn, Twitter, job boards, job aggregators (such as Indeed) and sites like Glassdoor.com can provide ample opportunities to research hiring managers, job openings across the industry, specific companies and the cultures within those companies. With a click of your mouse, you can research a company before an interview, so that you understand their corporate strategy and product suite. We will return to LinkedIn later in the book to discuss how to use it effectively.

Now for the dangers of social media. A 2012 survey commissioned by an online employment website found that 37 percent of hiring managers used Facebook, Google+ and other social networking sites to research job applicants. In the same study, 34 percent of hiring managers said they had come across something that caused them NOT to hire a candidate. Prior to starting any job search, make sure that your social media pages are free of any posts, comments or photos related to alcohol, drugs, sex, politics or anything that might cause any employer to think twice about hiring you. Be thorough! Check your activity log and use FB's "shared with" and "on timeline" filters to remove all questionable material. When in doubt, delete!

The same goes for your answering machine/voicemail messages and personalized email "signatures" or email addresses. If you email address is californiapartygirl@gmail.com, it is time to create a new email account.

Finally, "Google" yourself. See what you find. If there are problems, time to act. Sometimes, you find information is available that you wish were not. Or perhaps search results regularly bring up a criminal with the same name as you. If this is the case, you may want to contact one of burgeoning companies that focus on managing and protecting your online reputation. I recently read an article in a major business publication that mentioned one such company, www.reputation.com.

Step 5: Cover Letter

You will not need a cover letter for positions that you are pursuing with the help of a recruiter. That being said, your search may not involve recruiters for every position. If that is the case, you may want to take the time before your search begins to at least outline or create a rough draft of a cover letter. You may find that the process of preparing a cover letter will help you crystallize some of your thoughts and priorities as you begin your search.

A good cover letter should clearly state the following information:

- Why you are applying: It is best to focus on what interests you about the opening for which you are applying. Stating that you are miserable at work does not make for good cover letter copy. Remain positive!
- Why you are a fit for the position: Briefly summarize the skills you possess that match the open position. Sell yourself! Highlight how you can add value to the firm through your experience.
- Consider your audience: Explain how you meet the needs of the employer, not the other way around!
- Contact info: When closing the letter, make sure to include information regarding how to best contact you.
- Keep it simple: A half a page of text is best, certainly no longer than a full page.
- Call to action: End your cover letter with a request to meet or speak and thank them for their consideration.
- Reminder: Proofread! Spellcheck! Proofread again!

See Appendix for sample cover letters and résumés.

Step 6: Selecting Your Search Method

The next step is to determine how you are going to conduct your search. Determining the best search strategy depends on several factors including:

How Much Time Can You Personally Devote to the Search?

If you are currently employed, let's face it; you don't have a great deal of time to devote to a job search. Add to that studying for exams, a spouse/ significant other, friends, children, pets, a "life", and time becomes a very precious commodity.

For most people this means that you'll want to enlist the services of a recruiter. (Recruiter bias duly noted!) There are numerous firms, including Pinnacle Group, that specialize in actuarial search. Our services are free to you, the candidate, as our clients pay us to find actuaries with particular skills and credentials. As discussed in the next section of the book, working with an experienced recruiter will save you a huge amount of time and work, and will open up numerous avenues in the employment market unlikely to be available to you on your own. With one phone call to a recruiter, you will access information about a number of opportunities currently available that match your background, interests and geographic preferences. In addition, the recruiter will handle any additional research needed on the company, résumé submission and client follow-up. More on recruiters to come.

Recruiting firms do not have every job available, though we do have a very large number. Time permitting, you should also review the major job boards including the SOA and CAS websites for current openings. It will take more of your time but diversifying your search methods will increase your reach and potential for finding the right position.

Your Sense of Urgency

Several factors can influence your sense of urgency but there are a few common themes that make a person want to find a job more quickly. Examples include unexpectedly losing your job (fairly rare for actuaries), the desire to quickly exit an unhappy employment situation, or a personal matter that encourages you to find a new job "sooner rather than later". It's worth noting here, that if you do lose your job unexpectedly, urgency is imperative. It will likely take you a minimum of two months to find a new position and begin working at the new employer. This can put a significant strain on most individuals' bank accounts. Secondly, and perhaps more important, the longer you are unemployed, the harder it is to get a job. As time passes, rightly or not, employers begin to question why you've been out of work for so long; they begin doubting your rationale for why you were let go in the first place, and may begin questioning your desire to return to work and how up to date your skills are. It can become a very difficult situation and should be avoided if you can help it. As enticing as it might be to take a few weeks/months off, ("When else will I have this opportunity to travel the European continent?"), it should be avoided. You don't want to find that your eight-week sabbatical turns into an eight-month struggle to find a new job.

How Difficult Your Search is Expected to Be

As strong as the job market generally is for actuaries, job search efforts for a significant percentage of actuaries regularly take 6 months or more. This is not because these actuaries aren't highly skilled and accomplished. In fact, it is often quite the opposite; their degree of specialization and expertise often exclude them from consideration for positions for which they may be interested and capable of performing successfully.

If you are looking for a new position with increased responsibilities, you may need to be patient. Companies look to hire the person who most closely matches their current opening. If you are not an obvious match, the process will move forward more slowly for you than for those that do match. Here's an example: Let's say you are seeking a position with greater management responsibilities but you've only ever supervised one employee and a couple of summer interns. Then you learn that Dream Insurance Co is hiring for a position that matches your product and functional skills but it manages a staff of 5-7 employees. If you submit your résumé, you may find that it gets put in the "maybe" pile. In this pile, the hiring manager likes your background and may even want to conduct a phone interview with you. However, the hiring manager is hopeful that over the next few weeks, someone with more management experience will apply. As the search begins, the hiring manager may not want to take the risk that an "unknown entity" will be hired and ineffectively manage staff that he/she knows need strong leadership. After positions have been open for a few weeks or months, hiring managers often become more flexible and start entertaining candidates who are "close but not perfect". That, of course, is when you may find your opportunity to interview for this managerial role and convince them of your abilities to handle the position.

Actuarial Recruiting Firms (Warning, recruiter bias here!)

Overview of the Recruiting Industry

It is important to understand that recruiting firms vary widely depending on the industry/specialty area that they serve and the unique approach of individual firms. It is impossible to make broad generalizations simply because most recruiting firms are small, privately held companies which tend to reflect the personalities of their ownership as well as the dynamics within their area of specialization.

Unfortunately, as with so many industries, the level of professionalism runs the gamut from highly professional firms who care about both candidate and client relationships to "churn & burn" companies that are abrasive, unresponsive, or worse. The latter tend to operate in large industry segments where the candidates are highly interchangeable. Thousands of people can fill a marketing position in Indianapolis, for example, but only a handful of actuaries might be available for a life product development position at any given time. In professions as small and specialized as the actuarial profession, reputation in the community means far more than it might in other industries. For this reason, most actuarial recruiting firms take great care to be knowledgeable, pleasant to work with, responsive and effective. As will be discussed below (choosing a recruiting firm), you have plenty of options on which recruiting firms to select; so select wisely.

How are recruiters paid?

Most actuarial search is conducted on a contingency basis. This means that the recruiting firm is not paid unless they fill the position successfully. Similar to other "sales" positions, recruiters have to work very hard for everyone (candidates and clients) because they never know which candidates will be offered employment by which companies. One downside of this approach from the candidates' perspective is that some recruiters simply cannot resist putting pressure (sometimes heavy pressure) on candidates to accept a position if it is offered through their firm. While they may argue that their client ultimately pays their bill so they are working aggressively on behalf of their client, it is an approach that many candidates (and firms including Pinnacle Group) are not comfortable with.

Retained searches are occasionally used for actuarial search. These are exclusive searches where the client has agreed to pay a certain percentage of the fee upfront (usually one third of the fee) with the remaining fee to be paid upon the successful completion of the search. They are rarely used in actuarial search (other then for very senior level roles) for a variety of reasons. The primary reasons are: 1. Actuarial positions are hard to fill and clients are reluctant to give it to just one firm with limited reach, 2. Nobody likes putting money upfront unless there is a good reason. Nonetheless, some searches are offered to firms on an exclusive or retained basis. From the client perspective, they may want to limit the number of search firms to simplify the recruiting effort or may be conducting a search on a confidential basis.

The standard rate for actuarial search is 30% of first years' compensation (including sign-on bonuses and any bonus guarantees). This can vary but the rate typically does not drop below 25%. Recruiting firms do not bill clients on relocation expenses.

Should I Use a Recruiting Firm?

Given our fees, candidates sometimes wonder, would they would be more attractive to a company if they didn't work through a recruiter? It is a good question. It's one I'll seek to answer, but please forgive me if I am somewhat biased.

Client Perspective

What all hiring managers know, but many candidates do not, is that hiring managers ALWAYS want the best candidate available to fill their open job. It's not just, "who can do the job?" If it was, recruiting firms would have a much easier time placing candidates. Many other factors come into play; interpersonal skills, how much time the hiring manager has for training, etc. In addition, there are sometimes "internal equity" considerations (relative compensation and experience levels within the hiring department). The list is large and varies with each position and hiring manager. Despite, and sometimes due to these many issues, one candidate is typically the hiring manager's clear top choice during the recruitment and interviewing process. Given the choice between paying a recruiter fee for their top candidate or offering the position to a lesser candidate who is not working with a recruiter, the hiring manager will nearly always hire the top candidate. Most of our clients are Fortune 500 companies and they didn't get there by hiring mediocre talent. At a more granular level, the hiring manager is busy, the hire is a reflection on him or her, and therefore they want the best person for the job. In addition, the hiring manager is going to be spending a lot of time with the person and they want to have confidence in their abilities, including their ability to work well with others within the organization. A talented staff makes the hiring manager look better!

A second reason is that, due to the supply and demand factors in the actuarial marketplace, employers often expect that they'll pay a fee for a quality hire-and know that the rate of return on the investment is swift. Additionally, it's a form of outsourcing. Actuarial recruiters have very specialized knowledge and it would be far more expensive (and result in longer searches) to bring these recruiters in-house. Even if you save the company money by sending your résumé directly, you won't see the cost savings in a more attractive employment offer. While you might think the company could take the money they saved on recruiter fees to increase your salary, this is not the way it works. Compensation issues are determined internally using a variety of criteria such as level of position, compensation of similar positions within the firm/department etc., not by whether or not you were hired via a recruiting firm.

Candidate Perspective

Given my obvious bias, I would argue that working with a recruiting firm provides you with many significant advantages! Unless you are unemployed, you are unlikely to have the time to scour the marketplace for jobs that fit your skill set and interests. It is 100% of a recruiting firm's focus to match you with client positions that would be appropriate and of interest to you. Many actuaries, understandably, are "interested if the right job comes along" or "happy where they are" and not actively looking. Often it is these actuaries that our clients are looking for and we place people who "aren't looking" quite often! Regardless, it is very worthwhile to maintain relationships with a few select recruiters during your career to keep yourself informed of market activity as well as to benchmark your compensation from time to time.

For most active job seekers, using the services of a recruiting firm makes sense. Our services are free to you, the candidate, as our clients pay us to find actuaries with particular skills and credentials. There are numerous firms, including Pinnacle Group, that specialize in actuarial search. Additional benefits of using a recruiting firm are:

Time Savings

Working with an experienced recruiter will save you a huge amount of time and effort. We maintain extensive databases filled with company job postings, contact information and other relevant data. Quickly and efficiently, an experienced recruiter should be able to match your background, interests and geographic preferences to current actuarial openings. In addition, the recruiter will handle résumé submission and follow-up with each company. There is no need to research jobs on multiple websites or prepare cover letters for each company. We do recommend however, that candidates remain proactive in their own search efforts.

Getting Your Résumé Into the Hands of Decision Makers

A well-established actuarial recruiting firm will ensure that your résumé is seen by key hiring personnel as quickly as possible. We have connections with hiring managers that extend well beyond the <u>sendrésumés@abcinsurance.</u><u>com</u> addresses that are the only method available when submitting online. These company job portals are often a "black hole" for good résumés. When submitting online you are sending your résumé to human resources without any real opportunity for follow-up with either the HR representative or the hiring manager. You must wait for someone at the company to contact you, which often never happens. An actuarial recruiter will have the necessary contacts either within HR or the actuarial department or both. Moreover, we are expected to follow-up on the résumés submitted. It is part of our job and why the company has asked us to help them source candidates. As discussed above, if you submit your résumé yourself, you probably do not know who to follow-up with at the company. This is intentional on their part. Basically, they don't want to hear from you. They simply get too many résumés (for all different positions) to start fielding phone calls and emails from website applicants. Even if you do know who to call/email, it can be tricky to make sure that you are contacting them appropriately. It's a fine line between showing interest in an open position and either showing desperation ("I wonder why he wants to leave his company so badly?") or simply being annoying ("Ugh, another voicemail from Tom Schmoe!"). Recruiters are expected to call and if we call too much (which does happen in some instances) it might reflect poorly on us ("Boy, Mary Smith sure is pushy."), but you won't be impacted. It's the nature of our job.

In short, selecting the right recruiter (more on the selection process later) means that your search will go faster and you will be presented with many more opportunities than if you did not use a recruiting firm. Having the opportunity to interview with multiple firms should not only increase your odds of finding a position quickly but also help you ultimately select a position that best meets your interests and needs. Please keep in mind, however, that the job search process is characterized by "hurry up and wait". So regardless of how you search (with or without recruiters), it will typically take longer than you would prefer.

Smooth Interview and Negotiation Process

If there is one "best" reason to use a recruiting firm, it is to serve as a "buffer" during the interview process; facilitating communication between both sides and helping with negotiations of an employment offer. Many readers may think to themselves, "I don't need a recruiter to do that for me. I can handle that myself." And you're right, you can. However, it will often be to your disadvantage and may result in an offer never being made. I cannot stress this enough. I'm sure I speak for all recruiters when I say that you would be amazed at how sensitive both sides can be during the interview process and employment negotiations. In most instances, neither party knows the other very well. Miscommunication, misstatements, delays, incorrectly reading the "tone" of an email, and spousal issues are just a few of the pitfalls that may result in ruffled feathers on both sides, an offer never being made, or a less than optimal offer being made. I could fill an entire book with stories that would support this assertion. It is a delicate balancing act that our recruiters have to perform to get the needs of both sides met. At all levels of actuarial hiring, our role in facilitating and smoothing this process is invaluable.

Assuming the position and candidate are a match and both sides are interested, it is our job is to "make it happen". Recruiting firms are not compensated if both parties don't reach agreement on the terms of employment. Clear and timely communication between the two parties is critical. Typically speaking, both parties are not in agreement once the initial employment offer is made. There are questions that must be answered and concessions that must be accepted on both sides. As recruiters, we allow you to "speak your mind"; to really let us know, without any reservations or repercussions, what factors are necessary for you to accept the position. The same is true for our clients. Our client wants to fill this job with a great candidate. While they don't want to fill it at any just price, they want it filled (preferably quickly) and you have become an attractive candidate for hire. As they share their limits with us, we seek to encourage both sides to understand why the other side needs to increase or limit certain aspects of the offer. Through better understanding, comes compromise.

When dealing with sensitive issues such as your worth as an employee, relocating you and/or your family, reimbursement for relocation expenses, sign-on bonuses, annual bonus targets, long-term compensation incentives, promotional opportunities, job titles, job level, staff sizes, etc. people become very sensitive. Changing jobs is stressful and individuals are understandably more conservative in their thinking when contemplating the unknowns. A good recruiter will help eliminate as many of the unknowns as possible (on both sides) and therefore help alleviate the stress associated with the process. Ultimately though, both sides have to reach an agreement. If it fails because the two sides could not reach agreement, then so be it. Our goal is to make sure that it never fails because of a failure to communicate effectively.

How to Work Effectively With a Recruiter

If you are an actuary or an actuarial student, chances are you have received a call or email from a recruiter; possibly multiple calls and emails. While it may not always seem like it, these calls and emails are a good thing. Perhaps better stated, they represent a good thing. Recruiter calls indicate that your services are in demand from other employers. While there can always be "too much of a good thing", you should be pleased that recruiters are contacting you. Demand represents job security and the prospect of higher compensation in the future. If a recruiter calls at an inconvenient time, simply ask them to call back.

Selecting a Recruiting Firm

Assuming you are beginning a job search, how do you best select a recruiting firm? There are literally dozens of firms that recruit actuaries, though the number that specialize exclusively in actuarial search is far fewer. That should be your first criteria. You'll want to work with a firm that specializes in actuarial search. If they are a general insurance recruiting firm, they are unlikely to have the breadth of knowledge, client contacts and current job openings of a firm such as Pinnacle Group, which does specialize exclusively in actuarial search. Other firms that specialize in Actuarial Search in the US market include: Actuarial Careers, Andover Research, DW Simpson, The Jacobson Group and SC International. There are others of course but this would be a short list of our primary competitors for US placements. All have been in business for 15+ years, have sizeable staffs, and have generally favorable reputations in the marketplace.

Of primary importance when selecting a recruiter should be the relationship you have had with that recruiter over the months or years that you've been communicating with them. For the relationship to be successful, you must be comfortable that your recruiter is knowledgeable, skilled at what he/she does and interested in helping you find a position that meets your professional and personal goals. One rule of thumb that I believe is important is "If you like working with them, clients will like working with them." That is important. If you are not comfortable working with them, then I would suggest you do not. A good recruiter should be an effective representative for you to the client(s). They must be knowledgeable, professional, pleasant to work with and skilled at moving the recruitment process forward as quickly as possible. If you don't have confidence that they can achieve this for you then it is time to contact another recruiter. To that end, I think it is important to build relationships with a select group of recruiters. Most actuaries, once they have begun their actuarial career, stay in the field for decades. If this describes you, then you will likely make at least five career moves after starting in the profession. These job changes will require many hours of communication with your recruiter(s), possibly over several months. It is important to work with recruiters who respect your personal and professional needs, who advocate for you, and who effectively represent the needs of the client as well. In addition, they must be a sound career resource for you. They must be an expert in the employment market for actuaries. If they are not, then they cannot offer you prudent counsel during the search process. Trust me; this matters. Recruiter expertise leads to more and better opportunities for you. Over the years, that can represent a better career, better life-work balance and/or more financial security for you.

In summary . . .

A good recruiter should:

- Demonstrate that they are knowledgeable and networked
- Be trustworthy
- Be professional
- Be respectful
- Contact you with opportunities that are right for you
- Advocate for you in a job search process
- Represent client opportunities effectively
- Follow up with you after you have accepted a position
- Remain in contact with you over the course of your career

A good recruiter should not:

- Push you to pursue jobs you aren't interested in or qualified for
- Send your résumé anywhere without your express permission
- Call you or email you at work if you have asked them not to
- Pressure you to accept a position if you aren't happy with the terms of the offer

Once You've Selected a Recruiter:

What should you expect of your recruiter? Well, from all my comments above, quite a lot. But it is a two-way street. Recruiters will have expectations of you as well.

The most important responsibilities are to always maintain control over and organization of the search process. These are critical. You are the boss of where your résumé goes and when. Don't be bullied into submitting your résumé to a client or location that you are not interested in considering. If you are getting bullied, drop the recruiter. Also, never give the recruiter permission to send your résumé to any client without explicit prior approval. Some firms, will take advantage of the naivety of junior level actuarial students, for example, and blanket their résumé to a large number of clients without telling them where they are going to send the résumé. This is a situation you want to avoid as it represents a clear loss of control over your résumé. As for organization, you want to keep accurate records of where your résumé has been sent, on what date and via what method (name of recruiter, sent on your own, directly submitted on website, etc.). As a search develops, you will need these records. Your search may take months and you will want to make sure that you are not sending duplicate résumés to companies. It can reflect poorly on you and the recruiter and create conflict if the résumé is received from different sources (two different recruiting firms, for example).

Another essential part of working with a recruiter is honesty. All good relationships are based on both sides being honest with one another. If you have "warts" or "holes" on your résumé, there is no need to hide that from your recruiter. These items are very likely to be uncovered during the search process anyway. It is better to get everything out on the table upfront when you can better control how the information is presented. If it comes out later in the process, the client and the recruiter may think you were hiding something. Better to be honest right from the start. If these issues are addressed at the onset, a good recruiter will work with you and develop a search strategy that makes sense given whatever circumstances are presented. Below are some real life examples of situations presented to recruiters at Pinnacle Group.

- I never finished my undergraduate degree
- I was fired "for cause"
- I was arrested/convicted
- I left the company after only 2 months because . . .
- I may have a bad reference(s)

Despite these major issues, we were able to work with the candidates to find them positions that they were excited about accepting.

Honesty includes being 100% accurate and forthcoming with respect to:

- Every detail on your résumé
- Salary/Compensation (Many employers may verify compensation by asking for a previous year W-2!)
- Why you are looking for a new job
- Using more than one recruiting firm and/or submitting résumés on your own
- Being in the U.S. illegally

Other Search Methods

Job Boards

If you have the time to apply online and monitor the recruitment process, job boards may provide another good avenue for you to explore. Over the years, our clients have learned that qualified actuarial applicants are very difficult to find. As a result, many of our clients try to cover all bases by utilizing many possible avenues including job boards (e.g., monster.com, careerbuilder. com, theladders.com, soa.org, casact.com, etc.) You will find many actuarial jobs listed on these sites. If you have the time, it is worth reviewing some of the most relevant job boards. Please note, most of our clients use these sites in conjunction with actuarial recruiting services so you will see quite a bit of overlap. As mentioned throughout this section, you'll want to stay very organized so that you do not send duplicate résumés to the same company.

The effectiveness of job boards may be enhanced if your job search meets one of the following conditions:

- Entry-level
- Require H1B visa sponsorship
- Part-time
- Internships

Recruiting firms are hired by our clients to find experienced, full-time actuaries, preferably without other difficult issues that make the hiring effort more challenging. They are less excited to pay a fee for inexperienced hires or those that match the criteria above. As a result, you will find that recruiting firms have far fewer of these types of positions.

Please keep in mind the following items when using job boards:

- As an employed actuary, it is NEVER a good idea to post your résumé on a job board without hiding all data that can lead to directly to you. Your employer may be reviewing posted résumés; it is best for your job security that yours is not found. Most of the major job boards allow you to hide personal data. This is a must to avoid problems with your current employer and also for avoiding privacy/ identity theft problem.
- You'll want to include a cover letter to better explain why you are applying for a particular position.
- Do not expect to be able to follow-up with the company. As discussed previously, HR staffs are generally too busy to contact most online applicants (outside of an automated response letter) unless they are genuinely interested to speak with you.
- Stay organized; keep records of all résumé submissions

- If you are particularly worried about the privacy policies of job boards, I might suggest you read "Recommendations to Job Seekers on www.privacyrights.org.
- Never post your Social Security number (or list it on your résumé)
- Consider using a disposable email address
- Do not include references

Your Personal Network of Contacts

Time permitting, using your personal network of actuarial contacts might yield some potential "hits" in your job search. Many companies understandably encourage and monetarily reward employees for their referrals. For employers, it should be a good source for longer term hires. But for candidates looking for a job, it does have its shortcomings. For most people, it only provides you with a limited number of opportunities. If you are actively searching for a new job, this can be an effective method but should be used in conjunction other search methods to ensure you cast a wide net.

The success of this method largely falls to others. Even though you "have a friend at the company", employee referrals often have to fill out an online application and online résumé submittal. To a swamped HR recruiter, this submission looks exactly the same as an online submission except that you selected "employee referral" and listed the current employee's name instead of some other source such as "recruiting firm". The responsibility then falls to the employee to follow-up on your behalf. For the current employee, this is not easy. He or she is busy and the HR staff is as well. It is hard for them to be your advocate if they are only leaving a voicemail or email message. As a result, I believe that many companies, especially large ones, miss opportunities to hire "employee referrals". At small companies, where there is very little need for online hiring databases and other bureaucracy, employee referrals are much more effective because they are placed directly in the hands of the hiring manager. Finally, employee referrals work best if you cover all bases. By this I mean, submitting online (or following whatever HR recruiting process exists) as well as requesting that your friend or referring employee email your résumé (preferable with your cover letter) to the hiring manager. This can only be done if the hiring manager is known but at a smaller company, this is easier information to obtain.

LinkedIn

LinkedIn is a powerful networking and recruiting tool. You should use it. But use it carefully and under your own terms by controlling the flow of information. You can achieve this simply by managing the "Privacy Controls" and being very careful about what you post. With these controls you have the ability to disable activity broadcasts and limit the ability of others (including your boss) to monitor your activity feed, view if you've changed your profile, make recommendations or follow companies, etc. Be careful what you post! Posting that you are seeking a new job, or admitting to the same in the "Groups" or "Answers" while currently employed is typically not good for your employment status. Finally, I suggest you use a personal email address for your login. I think it's just proper protocol to do so. Plus, if you change jobs, you may lose the ability to log into your LinkedIn account if you used your company email.

Tips for an effective LinkedIn Profile:

- Make sure your profile is up to date with your current role and exam status. If you want people to access your profile and contact you for positions based upon it, include detail on what your current role entails. (You can use your résumé for content.)
- As referenced above, do make use of privacy controls so that your boss doesn't see if you are working on updating your profile for a job search.
- Join groups that will educate you on your professional interests or connect you with people who will benefit your professional career. (Alumni groups, groups of people who previously worked at a company you did, risk management professionals, etc.)
- Monitor your LinkedIn homepage periodically. There is a wealth of industry information, trending articles, job postings, etc. that will provide beneficial knowledge.
- Remember that LinkedIn is, above all, a *professional* site. The lines between professional and social media are becoming ever blurrier- have a clear line here and keep it professional. Your photo (if you use one) should not be you in a bikini or at your wedding; it should be a headshot of you in professional attire. You should assume that

people look at your LinkedIn profile prior to interviewing you, so your impression starts here.

Step 7: Applying for Jobs

There are a few simple rules to follow when submitting your résumé to companies for open jobs. These rules hold regardless of how you send your résumé to the company (e.g., recruiter, online submission, personal contact at the company):

a. Use a spreadsheet to keep track of where you sent your résumé, how you sent it, to whom it was sent (if known) and the date that you sent it. You will very likely need this information at a later time and you'll be glad you have it. By staying organized, you will minimize the chance of blunders such as sending your résumé to the same company from two different sources within weeks of each other.

b. Do not send duplicate résumés to the same company. Almost always, you'll only want to send a résumé to a company one time during a six (preferably twelve) month period. There are many reasons for this but the primary one is that you want to demonstrate your organizational skills. It is much better to follow-up with your recruiter and or the company directly (if you sent it to them directly, than to resend your résumé.

c. Utilize the same referral source for all your follow-up during the six to twelve month period after you originally submitted your résumé. For example, if two months ago you requested that your recruiter submit your résumé for a job at ABC company and you see a new job has opened that you'd like to also be considered for, contact that same recruiter and have him/her contact the company. If you do not submit your résumé to the same company in the same manner each time it can easily cause "conflict issues" regarding who deserves credit for attracting you to the company. This is not a good situation to be in the middle of, so it is best to avoid it.

d. Personal information—If you choose to submit your résumé directly on a company website, make sure to only provide the information necessary for the company to consider you for the job. Otherwise, your confidential search may become less so. Do not release any information that could create problems for you. For example, do not provide the company with your office phone number, office email address, or references' contact information. Companies may contact you at the office unexpectedly or may call your references unexpectedly. It happens with some frequency. Obviously, this can have dire consequences but can easily be avoided by use of your personal contact information.

Step 8: Follow-up with Companies

One of the most frustrating aspects of a job search is waiting to hear feedback regarding your résumé submission, interview, or a response during offer negotiations. Rarely are the delays on your end. Most delays are a result of actions or inactions on the part of the hiring company. Recruiters can definitely attempt to, and often do, move the process along at a faster pace. Inevitably, we will run up against issues that take time to work out. The reasons for delay are too numerous to list or even organize into categories. What is important is that you recognize that delays will take place and attempt to do what you can on your end to keep the process moving expeditiously. Working with a recruiting firm should help keep the process moving as quickly and smoothly as possible. As noted previously, recruiters are expected to follow-up on the résumé submissions, by you and the client. We are expected to discuss specifically what makes you a good candidate for the job, etc. We are expected to push things along to the extent possible, given the circumstances. But delays do happen, and they are as frustrating for your recruiter as they are for you.

5

THE INTERVIEW PROCESS

Goal of an Interview

I'm starting this section off with the "goal of an interview" because if you don't understand the goal, it's very hard to prepare properly to achieve it. Simply stated, your goal during an interview is to get to the next stage in the recruitment process. I'm not trying to be Machiavellian here, but if you don't perform well enough during the interview to get to the next step, then nothing else really matters. The result will be that the particular job and/or that particular company is simply not an option for you for the forseeable future. This is your career, so you want to keep as many options open as possible. Your goal is to get to the next step. To that end, you want to leave everyone you speak with impressed and happy that they took the time to speak with you. For this reason, there may be numerous items that are better not discussed until a later stage in the recruitment process. On most occasions, it is more appropriate to discuss items such as compensation, relocation reimbursement, study time, and other student program details later in the interview process.

Please do not read into this that you should be anything less than honest or candid. I am not suggesting anything of the sort. I am simply suggesting that there is a right and a wrong time to address everything during the recruitment process. The most obvious example of this concept is the issue of compensation. You should expect to be asked what your compensation is early in an interview process. Give a completely honest answer and move on. You may be asked to provide a copy of your W-2 and don't want any discrepancies. If during an initial interview, you bring up the fact that "I feel I'm underpaid" as a motivation for your search, this may send the wrong signal to the interviewer and end the process prematurely. Better timing for this conversation would be after the company has completed the interview process, become excited about your skills and most importantly, after they have made you an initial offer of employment. Before an employment offer is made, you have zero negotiating leverage. Once you receive an employment offer, you instantly have negotiating leverage. The company knows you better, they like you, and they can more fully appreciate your employment value. After receiving an employment offer, if you view the salary offer as too low, you can explain why you currently feel underpaid. In response, the prospective employer will hopefully be more inclined to find a compensation level that matches your expectations. Here, again, is where having a recruiter represent you in the process can be a real asset.

Preparing for an Interview

The best advice I can give anyone, regardless of what activity they are undertaking, is to "over prepare". This advice holds true when sitting for actuarial exams, planning a camping trip, making a presentation, and of course, interviewing for a new job. You never know what to expect during an interview or when camping in a national park, so it is best to "Be Prepared", as the Boy Scout motto famously implores. There are five primary areas that you must focus on to achieve this:

1. Job Responsibilities: In most instances, a job description should have been presented by the time you have reached the interview stage. Most job descriptions leave the applicant wanting more information pertaining to this position. The candidate must take a "leap of faith", recognizing that he/she will learn more about the specific responsibilities as the interview process unfolds. The reason for this is because it is very difficult to capture an entire job on paper. Hiring managers and HR are busy and they often rely on position descriptions that are recycled from years past. These position descriptions are tweaked or new ones are created new, but the best information regarding a position will be ascertained from direct conversations with the hiring managers, your recruiter and/or others within the company.

2. Company and Location Research: This process is so much easier today with the internet. It is so easy that you cannot be excused from doing research prior to your first interview. You'll want to research the firm's company overview, their products, their most recent company news and their financial performance. Annual reports, A.M. Best Reports, etc, provide a wealth of information; plenty for most actuarial interviews. If you are relocating for this position, it is a "must" that you research the city where the position is located. You will be asked why you are willing

to relocate, what connections you have to the city, if any, and what you know about the city.

3. Prepare Questions: While conducting your company research, you'll want to be jotting down questions to ask during the interview process. Obviously some of the questions are only appropriate for specific interviewers and/or at various stages in the interview process but this is a good time to create a list. The questions that you ask are important for two primary reasons. First, you are interviewing the company at the same time that they are interviewing you. Questions that you ask should help you better understand the position, the company and the overall opportunity. Second, the questions that you ask will be a reflection of you. Are the questions intelligent or do they show a lack of understanding? Do they get to the heart of the matter or are they trivial? Do they indicate that you have reservations or strong interest in the job? Do they indicate that you are changing jobs for the right or wrong reasons? Make no mistake about it, the recruitment process has been halted by candidates asking too few questions, or asking the wrong questions at the wrong time. You'll want to give considerable thought, in advance, to what questions to ask and even how to articulate them during the discussion.

I recommend addressing the following important questions near the end of the recruitment process, typically only after an offer has been made.

- Typical Work Hours: You will likely learn quite a bit about the expected or typical work hours during the in-person interview. If not, you'll have time <u>after</u> you receive an offer of employment to address this directly with your prospective boss.
- Compensation: Let the company bring up this topic, not you. Focus your questions on learning more about the non-monetary aspects of the job opportunity.
- Reduced hours or telecommute options: If the company brings this up as a selling point of the job then feel free to ask more about it. Otherwise, wait until you have received an offer to inquire about these matters.
- Benefits Details: Unless you have a particularly special consideration (e.g., a spouse or child with a severe medical condition) that must

be addressed right upfront, hold off most questions related to the company's benefit program and student program. Obtaining some general information is fine. The company will likely volunteer some of this information to you. But detailed questions about particular aspects of the programs should wait. You will have an opportunity after receiving an offer of employment to review all the details of the benefits information, ask questions, and negotiate certain items.

4. Review Your Résumé: Make sure you review everything written on your résumé (particularly special projects, achievements you've highlighted, etc.) It seems obvious but it is not always done.

5. Contemplate/Outline Answers to Common Interview Questions: Preparation and practice make perfect. If you want to impress an interviewer, you should take the time to contemplate and/or outline answers to standard interview questions (see next section). At some point during your job search, you will be asked many of these questions or similar questions. Taking the time to think through how you would best answer these questions will be very helpful. It is important that you "tell your story" and "sell yourself". Modesty has almost no place in an interview. Remember, it is your job during the interview to make sure that the interviewer has a clear understanding of your skills, abilities, and goals.

Common Interview Questions

Below are some commonly asked interview questions you should be prepared to answer:

- **Tell me about yourself.** If you are unprepared, this can be a difficult question to answer succinctly. Obviously, it is very open-ended. What you'll want to do is it narrow it down to "who am I professionally?" Once focused in this way, you'll want to highlight your professional qualifications, skill sets, and abilities. Emphasis should be placed on those qualities that are most relevant to the position for which you are interviewing.

- **What are your strengths?** There are no excuses for being unprepared for this question. The interviewer wants a straightforward answer as to what you are good at and how you can add value to the company. Concentrate on discussing three or four of your strengths and how they could benefit the employer. Ideally, these strengths will relate directly to one or more of the primary job responsibilities. Be sure to review the position description to see where your strengths overlap with the position requirements. Strengths to consider include technical proficiency, ability to learn quickly, determination to succeed, a positive attitude, leadership or management experience, and your ability to relate to people or achieve a common goal. Be prepared to cite examples.

- **What is your greatest weakness?** Again, you must be prepared for this question. Don't say you don't have any weaknesses. But you need to avoid "self-incrimination", Ideally, you'll discuss one (don't volunteer any more) weakness that can be viewed as a relatively minor issue or perhaps one that is the result of understandable circumstances. For example, you might offer the following weakness, "I'd say that professionally, my biggest weakness is with the pricing of variable products. Our company focuses on fixed products and I've had exposure to variable products only through…". Of course, this would not be a wise answer if you were interviewing for a variable pricing position so you'll want to know your audience. Be prepared to offer a second, more personal (rather than professional) weakness. Again, you'll want to consider how this weakness might be viewed in light of the needs of your prospective employer.

- **Are you happy with your career?** This question must be answered with either a "Yes" or a "Yes, but…" To reply otherwise will give the impression that you are either a malcontent or someone who has not properly guided his/her career along the appropriate path. You can use this question as an opportunity to state how this new position makes sense for your career aspirations. An example, might be something to the effect of, "Yes, I'm very pleased with my career to date but after X years at ABC Insurance, I've come to recognize that I need to take on greater project and people management responsibilities. This AVP, Annuity Pricing job appears to fit nicely with my background and my career goals."

- **What do you like about your present job?** I hope for your sake that this is an easy question. If it is not, then give it some hard thought. You must stay positive. The question is begging for a positive answer. If you give a negative one, you will likely have damaged your chances significantly.

- **What do you dislike about your present job?** This is a much harder question than the one above. It must be handled tactfully as the interviewer is trying to get at a key bit of information; basically, what functions or tasks do you like or not like or what other aspects of your current company's culture, organizational structure, etc do you dislike. All of this can be quite relevant to your new position. Again, preparation is critical for difficult questions such as this one. Be honest but try to focus on elements of the position or factors influencing the work environment that will not reflect poorly on you personally. For example, if you work at a smaller company, you might find that "I like my current position, but the actuarial staff at the company consists of only 5 employees, so I feel limited in terms of upward mobility."

- **Why do you want to leave your current employer?** This is an important answer to practice so that you articulate it clearly. Your response to this question should be thoughtful, concise and should clearly indicate that you have given your job search considerable thought. You'll want to state the factors that led to your desire to find a new position, such as greater challenge, more responsibility, greater long-term growth opportunity, etc. You don't want the interviewer to think that you are speaking to them on a whim or that a desire for more money is your primary motivator. Everyone knows more money is better than less, but it typically comes with greater responsibility or value-added to the firm.

- **What are your professional achievements?** Since your significant professional achievements should be stated on your résumé and/ or your cover letter, you need to be prepared to discuss them in an interview. This question can be a bit difficult for an actuarial student with only 1 to 2 years of work experience, but as you develop more experience you'll be expected to have greater accomplishments. For example: "My greatest achievement was to design and implement a new predictive modeling initiative that analyzes portfolio profitability and account pricing schemes." Ideally you should be able to highlight the benefits your achievement provided for you, your department, a product, etc.

Additional Questions to Review and Prepare For:

1. Questions focused on learning more about you personally/professionally, your ambition, attitude towards work, etc.

   - What are your career goals? Where would you like to be in five years?
   - How would your colleagues describe you? How would you describe yourself?
   - What are you looking for in your next position/company?
   - Provide an example of where you have shown initiative, taken on additional responsibilities or exceeded expectations at work?
   - Describe a situation where you found yourself overwhelmed at work. How did you resolve the situation?
   - How do you feel about working long hours and/or weekends?
   - What do you like/dislike about the actuarial profession? Why?

2. Questions focused on working with others, ability to deal with conflict, views about teamwork, managing personnel, etc.

- Do you prefer to work alone or in a group? Why?
- What are your strengths/weaknesses as a team member?
- Do you like managing people?
- What are your strengths/weaknesses as a manager?
- Describe a problem/conflict you faced at work and how you resolved it.
- What type of personalities do you find are most difficult to work with?
- Discuss a disagreement you have had with your co-worker. How did you resolve the issue?
- Discuss a disagreement you have had with your boss. How did you resolve the issue?

3. Questions focused on your perceived fit for the position, your ability to sell yourself, and as well as your preparation for the interview

- Why should we hire you for this position? What personal and professional skills can you offer this organization?
- What aspect of this job is most/least attractive to you?
- What do you know about the company (that you are applying to)?

Interview Types & Methods

To more effectively anticipate the interviewer's line of questioning, consider the interview type and method, primarily the following:

- Interview conducted by actuarial/technical manager versus human resources
- Interview conducted by telephone versus in-person

Actuarial/Technical Manager v. Personnel/Human Resources

Interviews conducted by actuaries or other direct hiring managers typically emphasize the technical requirements of the position at least as much, if not more than, personal characteristics of the applicant. Both are equally important, however. If you've gotten to the interview stage, the hiring manager has already pre-screened your résumé based on a number of technical requirements he/she believes are relevant for success in the position. As discussed throughout this book, the more senior the position, the more likely particular expertise will be sought, including management and general business acumen. Regardless of the level of the position you are interviewing for, you will also likely be faced with questions focused on the "personal side'. This line of questioning is more akin to what you will encounter during interviews with Human Resources representatives but these questions are regularly presented by anyone on your interview schedule. Regardless, technical and non-technical questions are equally important. I'm sure you have heard that the days of a "back room" actuary are gone. To a large extent they are and have been for a long time. In today's business world, an attractive new hire has to demonstrate the ability to effectively communicate ideas, work as a team member, problem solve, take initiative and multi-task, just to name a few. Non-technical skills such as these should be listed on your résumé and reinforced during the interview process.

First interviews, normally conducted by an HR representative via the telephone are sometimes a screening tool before an interview with the hiring manager. They simply want to gauge your basic communication skills, verify aspects of your résumé, inquire regarding relocation issues, etc. These screening interviews may or may not include difficult situational/personal questions. As with all interviews, you have to be prepared. They will also often ask for your compensation details, so be prepared for this.

Telephone Interviews

Telephone interviews provide employers with a cost-effective way of delving deeper into the details of your résumé as well as assessing your communication skills. They are convenient, and quicker than traveling to an office for an interview. It's important to take phone interviews seriously, though, as they can be challenging. As mentioned previously, be prepared! Have a copy of your résumé in front of you and be ready to discuss anything on it. If there is additional information not included on your résumé that you feel would help illustrate your fit for the position, feel free to discuss it. In addition, a client will want to know your reasons for considering positions outside of your current company. Make an effort to speak as clearly and concisely as possible. Hiring managers are interested in your communication skills as well as your technical ability. When you don't have the luxury of eye contact, communicating effectively can be difficult.

You should also prepare questions for telephone interviews. The answers may help you better understand the opportunity and it demonstrates an interest in the position. Finally, assuming you like what you hear during the conversation, it is important to express interest in the position and the company directly to the other person. End your conversation with a statement that clearly states your desire to move to the next step in the hiring process. An example of an effective statement might be, "Thank you for the opportunity to speak with you. From what I've learned during our conversation, this sounds like a very exciting opportunity. I would definitely like to learn more and interview further for this position." At the very least this provides you additional time to think about the information you just received without making a rash decision that could close doors.

Please note that it is best to avoid using your mobile phone during any stage of the interview process, if at all possible. Everyone is familiar with the shortcomings of mobile phones. If you want to make the best possible impression, a land line phone is strongly encouraged. In today's world, the majority of telephone interviews are conducted with at least one party on a mobile phone, but given the choice; it is best to avoid using them for telephone interviews.

In-person interviews

In-person interviews typically take about a half day. You most likely will need to take the entire day off from work to allow for travel and extra time in case the interview runs long. As discussed below, preparation and practice are critical to successful in-person interviews. In advance, you'll want to determine the strengths and experience most important to emphasize during the interview as well as the questions you'll want to ask. However, the first challenge you will encounter may be the employment application.

Employment Applications

Whether in advance of or when you first arrive for your interview, you'll almost certainly need to complete an employment application. It is very important that the employment application be completed accurately and with careful thought. The employer will likely refer back to this document at later stages of the recruitment process and your responses need to be consistent with information provided at this earlier stage.

The most vexing question on every employment application is "Desired Compensation" or "Minimum Salary Requirement". How do you respond to that question? Well, it is not easy. (Compensation is addressed specifically in the section on Offer Negotiation.) You need to handle this deftly. Ask for too much and they'll either decide you are only interested in money or they'll think they can't afford you and simply end the recruiting process. Ask for too little and you may be short-changing yourself and frankly not feel good about accepting the offer when it comes in below your desired level. Also, if you say to the company, "I wrote down currently earning X on the application but I'm seeking X+Y", it does not reflect well. Just as important, you have put yourself in a weakened negotiation position.

We frequently are questioned about how to respond to the compensation question when it is directly asked of you. Our responses vary widely depending upon the individual and the job but here are a few guidelines:

- Be truthful. Before making an offer, companies may request a pay stub or a copy of your W-2 form to verify your stated compensation.
- Be reasonable. In today's marketplace a 5-10% compensation increase is the norm.
- If relocating, recognize that companies are not going to pay you enough to compensate you for a cost of living (COL) increase if they are located in a higher COL area (not even close for cities such as NYC, Los Angeles, and San Francisco)
- If you feel you are underpaid, you might try to skirt the question by simply writing "competitive salary" but be prepared for the fact that you are likely to get a direct question about the actual number at some point. You'll want to be prepared to provide that number.
- If you recognize that you are overpaid and would be happy with a lateral move, you may chose to simply state your current compensation. The company may end up paying you more!

If you are using a recruiter, use him/her as a sounding board. Each circumstance is different so your recruiter should be able to lay out the possibilities for you. Ultimately, the choice is yours, but an experienced recruiter will provide helpful information that should allow you to adjust your compensation request appropriately given your needs and the limits of the job and/or company.

A second place to exercise caution is with the "Previous Employers" or "References" section. Assuming your current search is confidential, you'll want to be very careful about who you list as a reference or contact person. At the end of the application, you'll be signing an authorization and release form enabling the company to contact your references and perform other background checks. Ninety-nine percent of the time, reference checks are handled properly and your search remains confidential. But mistakes happen. To guard against this, I believe it is best not to list contact people until such time as it is appropriate. Companies would prefer to capture all the data at one time on the application, but again, I suggest you release only that information that you are confident will not jeopardize the confidentiality of your search.

Goal of an In-Person Interview

During the in-person interview process, you have one primary goal, which is to get an offer from the company. Yes, you want to collect information about the job and the company but if you ask the wrong questions or if you are too modest and don't sell yourself, you will not receive an offer. To repeat for the sake of emphasis, your goal is to the get the offer. Everything else is secondary. After you have received the offer then you can more confidently address any concerns that you have about the opportunity with the company. And more important, the company will be more willing to negotiate certain points with you since they are now excited about you joining their organization and have invested significant time and energy into the interview process with you. One more time, your goal is to get the offer.

In-Person Interview Tips

There is a huge body of literature available in your neighborhood or online bookstore regarding interviewing skills. I'll leave the detailed materials to these publications and other sources. That being said, before any interview, you may want to review the following tips as helpful reminders:

- Be Prompt - Know where you are going and when you need to be there. Your recruiter or company HR contact should provide you with directions and an interview schedule, if one is available. Show up on time. Do not show up too early. Contrary to some people's thinking, it does not make a positive impression. If you are early, wait until 5 minutes before you are due to arrive to check in.

- Be Polite and Gracious - From the minute you enter a company, be courteous to everyone you meet, from security to reception to someone who offers you a coffee. I can think of more than one story of candidates who were not advanced in an interview process because they were rude or not courteous in some way to a receptionist or assistant.

- Practice - As previously discussed, think about your interview ahead of time. Review your résumé thoroughly and prepare answers to questions that you are likely to be asked. If there are any questions that you have struggled with in the past, this is a great time to review them and prepare answers for them. Finally, if a friend or spouse is willing to "role play" with you, this is the best practice available. It will allow you to run a "dress rehearsal" of your answers, including making eye contact. Eye contact is very important. It shows confidence and allows you to make a more personal connection with the interviewer.

- Bring the Right Materials - Bring an attractive portfolio or briefcase, and paper and pen to take notes. Also, make sure to bring several copies of your résumé (one copy per interviewer plus a few extra).

- Dress for Success - Unless otherwise noted, wear your professional best. If possible, wear a nicely pressed, dark suit; insurance is still a conservative business. Iron your shirt, shine your shoes, style your hair and do not go overboard on the make-up or perfume! If the office is casual attire, make sure that you are "business casual" at minimum. You don't want to under-dress for an interview. Better to err on the side of "formality". Never wear sneakers, jeans, flip flops, short skirts or anything that might cause the company to question your professionalism.

- Be Confident - You know your skills and your experience. You are a talented actuary or actuarial student. Prepare thoroughly for the interview and be ready to sell yourself. You are a valuable commodity and you are in demand. So be confident!

- Discuss the Job Location - Companies are always looking for long-term hires. One common screening criteria used by companies is "ties to the area". The thinking of course is that those with family or other ties to the area are more likely to stay with the firm. You'll want to prepare for this line of questioning. If you have strong ties to the area, this is an easy question. If you do not, however, you'll want to research the area and be able to clearly explain either why are you considering the area or why you are considering the opportunity, regardless of the location. The point being, you want to reassure the company that you would be a worthwhile and long-term hire.

- Ask Questions - Keep in mind that while you are the interviewee, this is a mutual selection process. Asking questions will demonstrate your interest in the position and the company, and will also provide you with information necessary to make the right career decision.

- The interview "Lunch" - Often companies will have a potential peer (or peers) take you out for lunch during your interview day. This is not your time to let your guard down. While these people are here for you to talk to and ask questions about the student program, etc- they are still evaluating you and will likely be asked for an assessment of you following the lunch. Ask thoughtful questions but remain professional and focused. Be mindful of table manners; this is not the time to order a rack of ribs! And finally, hopefully this should go without saying, no alcohol.

- Clearly State Your Interest in the Position/Company - You would be surprised how important clearly stating your interest in the position is to the hiring company. If you walk out the door after the interview and the company is unsure about your level of excitement about the position, an offer may never be made. Employers want to hire people who want the job. The thinking is that those who are excited about working at the company will remain employed there for a longer period. Those who simply view the opportunity as a "paycheck" will be gone as soon as a bigger or easier paycheck becomes available. If selling yourself doesn't come naturally to you, make an effort to close each in person interview with a statement such as: "Thank you for your time. I am very excited about the position".

- Thank You Letters - We also recommend following-up an interview with a well-written thank you letter to those you met with during the interview.

Interview Feedback

Everyone wants prompt feedback from the company regarding how they performed during the interview. If you are using a recruiter, it is his or her job to share your feedback with the company and vice versa. This can happen within a matter of hours but unfortunately, may take many days. To understand why feedback can be prompt or painfully slow you have to understand human resources and the hiring companies. There are many things that slow down feedback. The primary reason is a hiring manager or human resources professional who doesn't understand the importance of prompt feedback. They get busy with other responsibilities and forget the fact that if the shoe were on the other foot, they would want to know ASAP how they did on the interview. Of course, there are many other reasons for delays such as:

- Collection of feedback from multiple people (The vacancy you have interviewed for has likely created extra work for the team, so they're busy!)
- Collection of feedback from senior management whose time is limited and whose priorities are such that hiring often comes second.
- Interviewers are traveling or on vacation
- Other interviewees are scheduled and they want to compare candidates before saying too much to any one particular candidate

If you are using a recruiter, he or she will likely be quite proactive in obtaining this information. But sometimes, recruiter calls and emails are not responded to until such time as the company has the information or has made time to share it. Trust me when I say that this will frustrate your recruiter as much as it will you.

If you are not using a recruiter, then you'll unfortunately have to be patient. You have a much more delicate balancing act to perform. You can't simply call in and say, "How'd I do?" You'll want to address the issue of advancing to the next step in the recruitment process in your thank you letter. If you have not heard back within a week, then you may want to place a carefully worded follow-up call or email to the contact that you feel is the most able to respond to your inquiry.

Learning whether or not the company would like to make an offer of employment can take hours, days or often many weeks. Typically, if the company is taking a very long time (two weeks or more) to make the hiring decision, they either have multiple candidates to interview or they've spoken with too few a number and feel they'd like to wait to see if another candidate might surface. They may or may not share this information with you and/ or the recruiter. It is always best if they do, so that your expectations are set appropriately, but this is not always done. In some cases, companies want to bring finalist candidates back for a final round of interviews.

How Best to Handle Delay

When delays happen during the interview process, it is only human nature for the candidate to start thinking along the following lines:

- "They must not have liked me that much."
- "I wish I had answered that question better."
- "They probably want someone with more _____ experience."
- "I thought it went well but I guess it didn't go as well as I thought."

As indicated in the statements above, delays almost always result in a plunge in the candidate's level of excitement and confidence. That's why we counsel our clients, often in vain, to make sure that they regularly communicate their interest in a particular candidate if delays in the recruitment process are expected. We have a saying here at Pinnacle Group, "Time kills deals". Delays on the part of the hiring company break the positive momentum of the recruiting process. Unfortunately, delays are common and in some cases they are not due to lack of interest. The key for you as the candidate is to stay positive and understand that almost by its nature, recruitment is a slow process. Does it have to be that way? No. Should it be that way? No. But more frequently than not, it is slower than expected. It is also important not to extrapolate one aspect of the recruitment process to the entire company or opportunity. It can be easy to fall into the trap of "If they can't get me feedback, then maybe this isn't a place I want to work". This is faulty thinking. As hard as it is, it is important to recognize that there are many factors delaying the process and that these are common. To the best of your ability, try to be patient and stay positive.

Thank You Letters

The purpose of the thank you letter is threefold. First, it is general courtesy to thank people for the time they spent with you. Second, thank you letters provide you with an opportunity to reiterate your interest in the position and company. Third, a thank you letter gives you a brief opportunity to address an issue if it presented itself during the interview. For example, the company might be concerned about your lack of direct managerial experience. You could address this in your letter by reiterating your direct supervision of interns over the past three years and recent MBA or professional management classes.

Thank you letters should be typed and proof read. Mail or email (perfectly acceptable) the letter within one business day of the interview to make the best impression. Keep in mind, whatever the outcome of your interview, the actuarial community is small; a positive and professional impression will benefit you in the years to come. If possible, send a thank you to everyone you met with at length. Spend the most time on the letter to the person who matters the most and with whom you had the most substantial discussion. Thank you notes should be brief, simple and to the point. Anything more and they have potential to detract from you as a candidate or raise questions about your writing style, professionalism, etc. Avoid leaving anything to interpretation and keep them SIMPLE.

Never use any texting or instant messaging short-hand "chat lingo" to communicate to a potential employer. "Thx for the chat! I wud luv to work 4 U!! :)" is not acceptable business communication, nor is the use of emoticons such as ☺. For that matter, you should not use short-hand language for any business communication. While some may overlook its use, many will not and it could result in a blown job opportunity. One final note on this topic, poorly thought-out messages from mobile devices are similarly damaging. If you want the job, demonstrate it by taking the time to send perfectly crafted emails, preferably from a home computer. Anything less, and you are at the mercy of the recipient to overlook your lack of professionalism. Bumr ☹.

Sample thank you letters are included in the Appendix.

References

As discussed in Section 4, you should have already contacted your references at the start of your search. After you receive an offer, it is time to check back with them. It is absolutely imperative that you re-confirm the fact that they can provide a <u>positive</u> reference. Make sure that they understand the importance of a positive employment reference. I strongly suggest you tell the reference something to the effect of, "Great, I'm really pleased that you can provide a positive reference. I'm very excited about this opportunity and I'm very hopeful to be offered the position. I'm sure your reference will be a help." The purpose of this statement is to say "Don't mess this up for me, I really want this job!" Occasionally, some reference providers try to provide both sides, the positives and the negatives. All I can say is "Ugh!" This type of "balanced" reference runs the risk of spending too much time on a small relatively minor issue when overall they feel great about the person that they are providing the reference for.

Make sure to tell the reference who might be calling or a least what company will be calling if you don't know exactly who will be making the call. This increases the likelihood of a quick turnaround, minimizing delay in the offer process.

After the reference is provided to the company, you should send the reference a thank you note. Email thank you notes are acceptable.

Offer Negotiation

This is a large topic area and a very important one as pre-employment negotiation of your compensation and benefits can make a significant difference in your bank account, job satisfaction and work-life balance. Frankly, it is best to negotiate these matters upfront before beginning your employment. Once the company employs you, your negotiating leverage drops. You will retain some leverage after you begin the position, but in most instances you'll find the company more receptive to your requests when they are "courting you".

Individual circumstances are so varied that it is impossible to address the topic of negotiation as completely as I'd like. However, this section will provide you with a framework for how best to approach your negotiation. Of course, you can enlist the aid of a recruiter. I cannot stress enough how helpful a knowledgeable and experienced recruiter can be in meeting the needs of both the candidate and the client. Negotiation of any kind is as much art as it is science. My goal here is to help you avoid the most obvious negotiating mistakes while "artfully" negotiating those items that are most important to you. Finally, you'll want to keep in mind that certain items are dictated by federal law and as such are non-negotiable.

Rule #1

The most important rule when negotiating an offer is to collect all the pertinent compensation and benefits information upfront. Reply one time to all aspects of the offer with the understanding that, if the company meets all your conditions, you will definitely accept the position. Bear in mind, there are several important parts to this rule. First, pertinent information is the information you need to make a final "yes/no" decision. Minor details can and should wait for later. Actuaries are detail oriented, but you don't want your potential employer to think that you can't see a good thing when it's staring you in the face. In other words, don't sweat the small stuff.

Second, once you have collected all the information needed to make a response, you'll want to prepare a thorough response to every important aspect of the offer. This response should include every modification you are requesting with specifics on how you would like it to be changed. For example, you might tell the client that you would "like to accept the position", that you are "excited about the opportunity", but request an additional $4,000 on the base salary, an extra $2,000 for relocation reimbursement, three weeks of vacation (as opposed to the two offered) and a start date of September 20th. This request clearly states everything you are requesting up front that would assure your acceptance of the offer. You don't want the hiring manager and human resources to be going back for multiple approvals. It will look as though you are "moving the goal posts". This might be the approach taken in the legal field or the world of politics, but it does not work in the business world. It frustrates the hiring personnel and reflects poorly on you.

Finally, it is important to communicate to the company (and/or your recruiter) that if the company meets your proposed conditions, you will absolutely accept the position. This is important for many reasons but the most important reason is that it maximizes your leverage. Simply stated, if a hiring manager knows exactly what it will take for you to accept his or her offer, you are more likely to get it. Alternatively, they know that if they fall short on meeting your demands, they run the risk of losing you and having to start all over again with another candidate. So, depending upon how reasonable your requests are, you are more likely to receive an improved offer if the company knows you'll accept the position.

Rule #2

Be flexible, reasonable, and responsive in all matters regarding the offer of employment.

No one wants to hire someone who is rigid or unrealistic in his or her expectations. During the interviewing process, the company will clearly get a sense of your personality. They will learn more about your nature during the job offer process. You want to make sure that the company does not begin to have second thoughts about offering you the job because, for example, you focus on nit-picky, small details rather than the overall opportunity or because you have unrealistic compensation expectations. Additionally, you'll want to be flexible about a wide range of issues including such items as:

- Receiving the job offer details over the telephone rather than in writing. (As a matter of policy, some companies don't put offers in writing until they have received a verbal acceptance.).
- Trusting the company when they tell you the "target bonus range is XX%". (Discretionary bonuses and other benefits specifics are rarely guaranteed in an offer letter.)
- Make yourself more readily available to speak with your recruiter or directly with the company. At this late stage in the process, you can no longer tell your recruiter "don't call me at the office" or "I'm traveling the next few days". Earlier in the recruitment process, issues can often be handled by email and delays are not as critical. But during the negotiation stage, letting the company know that this is a top priority for you is very important. If it's important to you, you have to find the time.

To echo the bullet above, be responsive and timely in your communication. In today's world, technology means you can work and communicate from any place, at any hour. Everyone knows this fact. To tell a potential employer that you can't get back to them for a couple of days because you will be attending a conference, for example, will send a clear message of "I'm stalling." This weakens your negotiating stance as clients begin to doubt your interest in their position.

Rule #3

Recognize that your circumstances are unique and not likely to change much in the short-term.

I'm sure that I speak for all recruiters and hiring managers, including recruiters at D.W. Simpson, when I say that we universally cringe when we hear, "According to the D.W. Simpson (or Bureau of Labor Statistics) salary survey, I should be earning between X and Y in compensation." Or this gem, "a friend of mine just took a job and got a 25% pay increase and I'm looking for something similar." Unfortunately, your current employment and compensation circumstances are your circumstances, and no one else's. One person's good fortune does not translate into good fortune for you. For some, this is difficult to accept. Perhaps they view actuarial and other business skills as a commodity with financial arbitrage forcing employers to offer compensation to those in the profession within a narrow range. Or perhaps, like 80% of most individuals, those in the actuarial profession rate themselves as "above average". Regardless of the reason, some people have unrealistic expectations of how the market values their services. These people are likely to be disappointed with the compensation and benefits offer that they receive. Most likely the offer they received was competitive vis-a-vis the marketplace. If they received three more offers from similar companies, more often than not, the offers would be within a narrow range of one another.

It is important during the negotiation process to weigh the job opportunity offered to you in the context of what is the best decision for you at this point in your career. Over time, you can better position yourself and make material improvements to your employment marketability, thereby boosting your worth in the marketplace. But right now, with an employment offer on the table, you must consider your current circumstances, recognize that they are different than someone else's, and make the best decision you can. I wish I could tell you differently.

Rule #4

Recognize that the "perfect offer" and "perfect timing" do not generally exist.

As disappointing as it may be, you will almost always be giving up something when you change jobs. Companies' compensation and benefits policies are different, their job titles and organizational structures are different, and their cultures are different. This all adds up to recruiting and employment practices that will benefit you in certain ways but may detract from the opportunities in other ways. No one wishes this statement was false more than your recruiter. It would certainly make our jobs much easier if employment offers were better in every way. Unfortunately, there are gains and losses with every employment offer. They are typically better overall, sometimes considerably so, but some aspects of the opportunity will still be missing. I like to use the analogy of buying or renting a home or apartment. It doesn't take the buyer or renter long to realize that there are pluses and minuses with every housing option. Very rarely do you find a home with a better location, more living space, all new appliances and fixtures for less money than a smaller home in need of repair in a less desirable location. Each housing option must be compared and sometimes it's hard to know which is better. When you find the right property for you, however, you'll know immediately and you'll be excited and ready to make the move.

Similarly, if you have been interviewing with two or more companies, you'll likely have interviews proceeding at different rates. One company may be making you an offer while another company is just setting up a first telephone interview. It would be great if the timing would work out in such a way that you could compare two offers simultaneously and make a decision, but this does not always happen. Even if you successfully stall one company a bit and accelerate the process at the other company, you may have to make a decision based on incomplete data. You may know all the details of one job offer but don't know if another job offer is coming and whether the second offer will be better or worse than the first one you are currently considering. There is no simple advice that anyone can give you in this situation. It's an imperfect situation and sometimes the best advice anyone can offer is to make the best decision you can based on available information. Some people might call this "going with your gut".

Rule #5

Negotiate What You Can

As mentioned above, all employment offers vary based on the particular candidate, job, and company. Guidelines for negotiable items are difficult to outline. That being said, the following list represents thoughts on the major items that most candidates will find as "negotiable" when presented with an employment offer.

- Annual Compensation—For most actuaries, a 5-10% increase for a job change is common. If you are offered more, great! However, don't expect much in the way of cost of living (COL) adjustments. See Rule # 7 for more on COL adjustments. Keep in mind that while you may feel you deserve more, the company has to consider "internal equity" or the rate of pay of others at your level that currently work at the company. If they offer you more than someone in a similar position that has worked at the company for a number of years, they risk creating a multitude of problems internally including, but not limited to, employee morale and retention, and budgetary problems. Also, companies typically do not want someone to take a position simply because it represents a 20% pay increase. They would rather recruit an actuary who is excited about the job and the 5-10% pay increase than an equally qualified actuary who "kind of" likes the job but is really excited and motivated by the 20% pay increase. The client's fear is that the latter is not a long term hire prospect.

- Relocation Reimbursement—Again, this area can vary from firm to firm but most often it is based on the level of the employee. For example, junior level employees may receive lump sum relocation expense packages between $2,000 and $5,000 (gross, before taxes). For more senior employees, packages worth $25,000 - $35,000 are common. Regardless of the size of the relocation reimbursement package, the more generous offers will reimburse the new employee for moving related expenses rather than providing a lump sum payment. Reimbursement is more generous to the new employee because reimbursement of direct moving expenses has fewer tax implications than a lump sum distribution, which is taxed as income.

- Start Dates—For most companies, sooner is always better but if there is a good reason, start dates can be pushed out as many as 8-10 weeks from the acceptance dates. Good reasons may include a pre-planned/pre-paid vacation, the need to transfer an H1-B visa, or waiting a few weeks to receive a substantial annual bonus payout. Reasons for significant delay that will not reflect well on you and should therefore not be requested may include taking time off "because I want a break", waiting for your kids to finish the semester (you go first, your spouse and children will have to follow later), or because you want extra time to study for an upcoming actuarial exam.

- Sign-on bonuses—Don't expect a sign-on bonus "just because". Sign-on bonuses are used for one of three reasons. First, to entice junior hires to take the position and/or to cover moving expenses. Second, to compensate employees who may be walking away from sizeable annual bonuses or other long-term compensation. Third, to make up for deficiencies in the new hire's first year compensation. Companies universally frown upon candidates who ask for a sign-on for no reason. They look at it as a "money grab" which is often exactly what it is. As with all aspects of the offer, it is best for the candidate to justify the request, even if the justification is that "I want more money." For example, a candidate could state the following, "My current salary is X. You have offered X + 5%. To accept this offer, I feel I need to earn X + 10% in my first year. Could you offer a sign-on bonus to make up for the difference?"

- Other Long Term Incentives—Not to be confused with non-executive retirement plans such as your 401k or Defined Benefit plan, other long-term incentives are typically benefits such as stock options or stock grants that are given annually based on measured criteria (most often with a vesting schedule to incentivize the employee to remain with the company). Companies do not have federal non-discrimination regulations guiding these types of long-term incentives, so these benefits can often be negotiated upfront. The level of your position will largely determine the range you fall into as well as how much flexibility the company may have to "sweeten" the employment offer. You can often negotiate the dollar amounts but typically cannot negotiate the vesting schedule except at the very highest levels of the corporate ladder (SVP at a minimum).

- Vacation / Paid Time Off—This benefit typically has limited flexibility. For the most junior hires, don't expect any flexibility. As you progress in your career you will almost always find 3 weeks as the minimum amount of vacation time with more weeks negotiable, depending upon the company. If you are offered 4 or more weeks, great! Some companies offer paid-time-off (PTO) which combines vacation days, sick days and "personal" days. PTO normally will begin no lower than 15 days, with 20-25 days PTO more commonly offered. If you are in the unfortunate situation to be offered no more than two weeks of vacation, you may have a couple of options.

First, take a few days off before you start the new job. Second, talk directly to your prospective manager. It is the Human Resources manager's job to enforce the company policy while the manager may "look the other way" if you are performing well. He/she may be well aware of the issues presented with only two weeks of vacation and will consider flexibility if you are a valued employee or desirable candidate.

- Title—Titles vary company to company. For the most part, I would counsel junior level employees to largely ignore them. It usually has no bearing on your compensation or marketability. Getting the best work experience and the most responsibility is key, not your job title. Once you achieve your Fellowship or perhaps reach the Director or Assistant Vice President level, titles become more important. Again, depending upon the company, reaching this first "officer-level" position can lead to more generous bonus pools and other benefits. But even at this level, the meanings of titles vary. The actual total compensation and position responsibilities that you hold are much more important to your employment marketability than the official title of your position. Stated differently, if the dollars are right and the job is right, tell your ego to take a vacation. One final point; title inflation is common in positions that have significant client contact such as reinsurance. At most reinsurers, for example, there are a disproportionate number of Vice Presidents and Senior Vice Presidents as compared to primary insurance.

Rule #6

Recognize that Certain Items are Non-Negotiable

- Retirement plans—Defined benefit and defined contribution plans are regulated by the federal government. Non-discrimination testing and other federal regulations mean that these benefits are basically non-negotiable. Of course, if you negotiate a higher salary or title, you may fall into a more generous pay grade and therefore you may achieve better retirement benefits.

- Medical, Disability, Dental, Group Life and Vision benefits—Similarly, most actuaries (except perhaps at the highest levels of management) will be treated exactly the same way as other employees in relation to medical and non-medical benefits. There may be some modest variation based on pay grade/level but again, these are largely non-negotiable.

- Study program details—It almost goes without saying that all actuarial students will be treated the same with respect to student programs at their companies. Most companies try to offer competitive study time programs. The key during the interview and negotiation process is to determine if students within your future department actually get their allotted study time and how much flexibility you can expect in determining what time off you can actually take given the needs of the department.

Rule #7

Cost of Living (COL) Adjustments Are Modest

This may come as a surprise to many younger actuarial students but companies will not fully compensate you for working in a higher COL area. There will be a modest wage premium but it will not be enough to offset the higher housing costs, taxes, or other factors. This often does not make sense to candidates but it is "good policy" for employers. The hiring company wants you to locate to their city because you want to move to their city, not because it is financially attractive to do so. The rationale is that employees with ties to the area will be more likely to stay at the company. It is important to note that often in higher COL markets such as NY, Boston, and Chicago, there are more employers thus greater professional opportunity.

A final note on COL: the best research is typically not online. Years of dealing with this issue has demonstrated to us here at Pinnacle Group that rents and home prices online tend to be much higher than you may actually need to pay. To find out the true cost of living in an area, it is best to talk to someone who has recently been house or apartment hunting in the area or do it yourself in person.

A Recruiter's Help

As I mentioned at the start of this section, a knowledgeable and experienced recruiter should be a huge asset to you during this process. Your recruiter should help you develop an upfront negotiating strategy given your particular circumstances, professional goals and personal needs. The above listed "rules" are important to know and understand but you will still find a recruiter to be an effective advocate for your needs and wishes during the negotiating process.

How to Accept a Job Offer

Accepting an offer of employment should be exciting for you and for the hiring company. The most important facet of accepting an offer is to make sure you communicate your enthusiasm to the company.

In the perfect scenario, you will accept the offer in a timely fashion (after negotiations). This is one important way that you communicate your high level of interest in the position. If you attempt to delay giving an answer to the company while you wait to see if you are going to receive a competitive offer from a different company, you send a clear signal of "I'm not sure I want to accept your offer". This is less than ideal but can certainly be overcome if handled properly. Here again, a recruiter can help with the communication process. An effective recruiter will work with the company to see that they are putting their best offer on the table and also make sure that the timing will work out for both parties. If the timing will not work out, it is the responsibility of the recruiter to make sure both sides know what timing will work and urge both sides to be flexible.

How to Decline a Job Offer

How offers are declined is more important than how they are accepted! The actuarial profession is small. It may not seem small when you consider that there are approximately 30,000 actuaries in the U.S. but as I'll illustrate, geography and specialization quickly shrink the universe. For example, let's analyze a large metropolitan area such as New York City. Our database shows approximately 3,000 actuaries and actuarial students in the NYC area. But if you are a life actuary, for example, then that number drops to 850. And if you would rather be a life actuary in New Jersey than in New York or Connecticut, that number drops to 300. That is a small number in a very large city. For this reason, it is very important that you leave people with a positive, professional impression of you before, during, and after the interview process. It is quite likely that your paths may cross in the future and you'll want to keep as many doors open as possible.

When declining an offer, you'll want to effectively communicate a positive rationale for declining. This is not an oxymoron. Here are a few examples:

- "I like the company and the department, but this particular job is not right for me at this time. I hope that I can be reconsidered for other openings in the future."
- "Unfortunately, I have accepted another position. I had hoped to have the opportunity to interview further for this position but, I had to make a decision about this company sooner than I would have liked. Opportunities at your company sound exciting. I hope we can remain in contact in the years ahead."
- "Unfortunately, I cannot accept this position with the compensation as offered. Perhaps, in the future, we'll have the opportunity to talk again about different positions with XYZ company."

Three of these examples explain, in a positive manner, why you cannot accept the position. The rationales are sound and each example clearly communicates to the company that you have a positive impression of their organization and that you are open to discussions sometime in the future. Even if you were less than impressed by one facet or another during your interaction with the company, it still makes sense to remain upbeat about possibilities in the future. In the case of a declined offer due to unacceptable compensation, such as the third letter, it is still best to be polite and leave the discussion on a positive note. It helps to maximize your future employment options. In all cases, you should thank the company for the offer and the time they spent with you during the interview process.

Counter Offers

After you "give notice" or state your intention to leave your employer, they may ask you to consider a counter offer. Counter offers are improved employment terms (or promises to improve employment terms), such as a higher salary and/or a near-term promotion should you decide to stay at the company. They can also include such non-monetary items such as an increased title, a potential change in role or a unique training opportunity. Counter offers do not happen very often, but they do happen. I would estimate they occur approximately 5% of the time in the actuarial profession. However, when you are giving your resignation notice, you'll want to be prepared for the company to "counter". To help you prepare, here are a few thoughts:

- Remember why you wanted to leave in the first place. For most people, their reason for leaving cannot be fixed with a counter offer, although all circumstances are different. In particular, think long-term (at least the next 12 months). Is this counter offer a temporary fix for you and your current employer? If it's a bandage, these same issues will likely resurface again.

- Do you expect long-term opportunities to be better at the new company or your current company?

- How will the counter offer change your workplace environment if you stay? It's always hard to know with certainty but you must have some sense of it from your time at the company. Do you think that your company is simply buying time to replace you? Will you be "welcomed back" without resentment from your manager or others within the firm? Will they continue to view you as a trusted "team player" and as someone committed to the long-term goals of the company?

Generally speaking, approximately 50% of people decline counter offers. Anecdotal evidence suggests a much higher percentage decline in the actuarial profession. I don't find this surprising when you consider what a difficult situation it is for the employee. First, the employee often has strong feelings of guilt or disloyalty once they've given notice. It is not a comfortable feeling. Second, if a counter offer is made, they find themselves in a quasi-negotiation situation with their manager, perhaps their manager's manager and human resources. Often word is leaked out and the whole office is talking about the employee and the counter offer. Ugh! In this situation, true negotiation is difficult. The company wants the employee to accept their counter offer but it's not particularly pleasant negotiating for more money or a promotion under these stressful circumstances. Perhaps this is why a Wall Street Journal survey showed that 93% of those people who accept counter offers leave within eighteen months[1]. It is my hypothesis that these individuals accept a counter offer that is inadequate, either financially, in responsibilities gained, or in terms of any of the other motivating factors that lead to the individual's job search in the first place. The grass is indeed sometimes greener.

(1) This is a widely quoted survey but I could not locate the original article. According the websites such as www.vault.com, "In a survey done by the Wall Street Journal, over 50 percent of individuals receiving counter-offers after turning in their resignations accepted them. Within eighteen months, 93 percent of those accepting counter offers had left, some voluntarily and some fired. All of the remaining 7 percent were actively seeking new employment."

6

TIPS FOR A SUCCESSFUL
ACTUARIAL CAREER

A career as an actuary is very demanding. Passing the actuarial examinations is grueling. Life, in general, can be a juggling act as you seek to keep all the balls in the air. With competing demands on your time, how do you ensure that you have a successful career? I'd like to suggest several "difference makers" that I encourage you to consider:

Difference Maker #1—Read General Business and Industry Publications

The Wall Street Journal used to run an ad years ago about a young man who read the *WSJ* every day. As the years passed, the ad suggested, the knowledge he gained from reading the *WSJ* helped lead to his considerable success. I would argue that there is truth in advertising! Given the rigors of the actuarial career and the considerable hours dedicated to pass the actuarial exams, it is understandable that many actuaries do not regularly read major general business publications such as the *WSJ* (you can substitute *The Financial Times* for more international coverage), *Bloomberg-Business Week*, or *The Economist*. This is a mistake. If you want to advance in your career, reading these three publications will help you in many untold but significant ways. General business publications such as these broaden your learning, provide you with insights on industry trends, and better prepare you for management and senior management positions. I stress these publications because your local paper's business section is not robust enough. This is true even if you live in a major city such as Los Angeles, Dallas, Chicago, New York or Boston. These cities all have fine newspapers but they are not "difference makers" in your career. And by all means, you should absolutely continue to read industry trade publications such as *The Actuary* and *Contingencies*.

Difference Maker #2—Develop Your Communication Skills

Effective communication skills (writing, speaking, and presenting) are critical to your career advancement. I repeat, critical to your career advancement. If you want to take on more responsibility and earn more money, you must invest in your communication skills. This is true if you are from Omaha or Mumbai. It takes many hours of dedicated practice to dramatically improve your communication skills. A business writing course, or better yet, multiple business writing courses, would be an excellent place to start. It will absolutely open more career options for you.

Finally, presentations are fixtures in companies, large and small, consulting or insurance. If you haven't made a presentation yet, chances are that you will sooner than you know. Effective presentations can make the difference in your career, especially when they are combined with strong writing and speaking skills. The content of your presentation, especially in the actuarial field, is most important. However, how you deliver the presentation will impact how you are viewed within the company. A strong presenter will come across as confident, articulate and knowledgeable. Presentations are arguably the easiest type of communication skill to master, though mastery of any subject requires concentrated energy and practice.

Many large companies have large training & development functions that offer an array of communications courses. Seek your training department out and see what is available to you. Outside of your employer, it is not difficult to find local presentation skills workshops/seminars. I strongly suggest you enroll in one or more of them throughout your career. Think of it this way: why would you take golf or tennis lessons but not a course that will help you advance in your career and earn more money?

Suggested avenues to improve communication skills:

- Business writing courses
- Presentation skills training (with video)
- Public speaking (Toastmasters, etc)
- Sales training (for those in consulting roles requiring revenue generation)
- Effective conference call and voicemail training

Difference Maker #3—Work Hard Toward Your Goals

You must set short- and long-term professional goals for yourself. And then work hard, very hard toward achieving them. My father, the son of a coal miner, once reflected about the success he enjoyed in his career. He said that "the harder I worked, the luckier I got." Luck? I don't think so.

It was the first half of that statement that led to his success. If you aren't willing to work harder than the people around you, then you can't expect your career to outperform theirs. If you want greater responsibility, greater compensation, and faster promotions, you have to demonstrate your capacity to handle your current responsibilities in a manner that leaves colleagues and managers certain as to your abilities now and even more so in the future. Each assignment that you undertake is a reflection on you and your potential. There is no mystery to this formula: Goals + Hard Work = Success.

Difference Maker #4—Semi-Annual Career Check Ups

The annual performance review is a fact of life in corporate America. It is a tool that management uses to review your performance, but just as importantly, it is a development tool for you. After your annual review with your manager, ask yourself the following 2 simple questions:

1. Is your manager indicating that you are performing at a high level, a level necessary for you to achieve your professional goals?
2. Are you actively following the advice in this section of "difference makers"?

I hope the answer to both questions is "yes". If not, then as I stated in Difference Maker #3, you've got some hard work ahead of you. After meeting with your manager, put an entry in your calendar for 6 months out. Annual self-reflection is not enough; you should review your goals, performance, and plan for achieving your goals every six months.

Difference Maker #5—Avoid Too Many Employer Changes

All things being equal (which is never the case), it is better to create opportunity within your existing employer than to more to a new employer. Once you've begun your career as an actuarial student, you'll have many opportunities to change employers. This doesn't mean that you should always do so. You should view any potential employer change within the prism of how it will help you achieve both your short- and long-term professional goals. Obviously, there will be personal factors that come into play as well. Make sure you have thoroughly explored your options within your current employer. Bear in mind, too many employer changes can create "red flags" that future employers will scrutinize for many years.

Difference Maker #6—Develop and Nourish Your Professional Network

Your professional network is of paramount importance as you advance your career. Focus on building your network within your employer; get to know people in other parts of Actuarial or other departments. Leave them with a positive impression of your work quality and work ethic and they may think of you when advancement opportunities arise. If you change employers, keep your network at your previous company intact by using LinkedIn. Attend conferences and networking events such as local actuarial society meetings; talk with people you meet and follow up with them to remain in professional contact and discussion. The actuarial profession is small and you will undoubtedly find that a robust network will serve as a great asset to your career over time. For consulting, this network is critical.

7

APPENDIX

Sample Cover Letter: Entry Level

John Smith
25 Edgevale Road
Cleveland, OH 43443
(216) 216-4089
john.smith.3@gmail.com

June 25, 2013

Tom Miller
Recruiting Specialist
XYZ Insurance Company

Dear Mr. Miller,

I am a recent graduate with a Master's Degree in Applied Statistics and am eager to begin my career as an actuary. I believe that the skills I have developed through my employment experiences and educational training will make me an asset to the company I work for.

The combination of technical analysis and emphasis on communication attracted me to the actuarial profession. When I decided to come to graduate school to study applied statistics and begin writing actuarial exams, I envisioned completing my studies and working in a dynamic and fast-paced environment which would offer me a rigorous training ground as I develop in my career. I have researched the impressive actuarial student program at XYZ Insurance Company and feel it matches well with my professional goals.

I would appreciate having the opportunity to discuss how I can contribute and be an asset to XYZ. I look forward to hearing from you and welcome any questions you may have about my background.

Thank you for your time and consideration.

Sincerely,
John Smith

Enclosure: résumé

SAMPLE THANK YOU LETTER

7 Apple Court
Eugene, OR 97401
503-555-0303

December 10, 2012

Mr. Steven Page
XYZ Insurance Company
5 Main Street
San Francisco, CA 94102

Dear Dr. Page:

Thank you so much for taking the time to interview me today for the Associate Actuary position.

I felt an immediate rapport not only with you, but with the entire team that I interviewed with. I am convinced that I would fit in well as a member of the department and contribute my skills and talents for the benefit of XYZ Insurance Company.

I am very interested in this position and can make myself available for any further discussions of my qualifications that may be required.

Again, Mr. Page, I very much appreciate you and your staff taking so much time to talk with me about this exciting opportunity.

Sincerely,
John Oakley

SAMPLE THANK YOU LETTER

12 Winding Brook Lane
Oakdale CA, 55555

April 5, 2013

Barbara Davis, Vice President
XYZ Insurance Company
1212 West Drive
Los Angeles, CA 55555

Dear Ms. Davis:

I enjoyed speaking with you today about the assistant actuary position at XYZ Insurance Company. The job seems to be an excellent match for my skills and interests. The creative approach to product development that you described enhanced my desire to work with you.

In addition to my enthusiasm, I will bring to the position strong writing skills, work ethic, and the ability to encourage others to work cooperatively with the department.

I appreciate the time you took to interview me. I am very interested in working for you and look forward to hearing from you regarding this position.

Sincerely,
John Smith

SAMPLE THANK YOU LETTER

Jerome Connolly
1 North Drive Apt 205
Boca Raton, FL 33486

February 18, 2013

Mr. William Chen
The XYZ
212 President Dr., Suite 300
Boca Raton, FL 33486

Dear Mr. Chen,

Thank you for taking the time to discuss the senior actuarial assistant position at The XYZ with me. After meeting with you and learning about the company's operations, I am convinced that my background and skills match well with your needs.

I appreciate the time you took to talk with me about the job responsibilities and the company. It gave me insight into why The XYZ has been a success. I feel I would be a good fit for the position, especially given my experience in actuarial analysis.

In addition to my experience from my previous actuarial positions, I feel I bring a strong work ethic and team-oriented attitude, both of which I know to be essential to success. I look forward to hearing from you about the position.

Sincerely,
Jerome Connolly

THANK YOU LETTER: TOPIC FOLLOW UP

7 Shawnee Road
Short Hills, NJ 07078
201-555-0303

June 10, 2013

Ms. Tess Bonwitt
B&B Insurance Company
1010 Madison Avenue
New York, NY 10021

Dear Ms. Bonwitt:

I'd like to thank you for the time you spent talking with me about the Actuarial Analyst position open at B & B Insurance Company. I am very excited about this position and confident that my actuarial training equips me well for the job.

I neglected to mention during the interview that last summer I attended a three-week intensive seminar on Access. I know the job description mentions the ability to use Access, and I wanted to make sure you knew that I am extremely well-versed in the use of this software. Please contact me if you have any questions about my ability with this program or about any of my other qualifications.

As you know, my current position at XYZ provides an excellent background for the actuarial work you described.

I look forward to hearing from you soon about the position, and I again thank you for meeting with me.

Sincerely,
John Oakley

SAMPLE THANK YOU LETTER- TOPIC FOLLOW UP

15 Oak Avenue
Newtown, NY 10101

September 15, 2012

Martina Bosserio
Manager, Product Development Dept.
Miller Insurance
1520 Widget Drive
Metropolis, NY 10021

Dear Ms. Bosserio,

I enjoyed the opportunity to meet with you and have a brief tour of Miller
Insurance. The high level of creative energy among your staff, as well as their
personal pride in the company's products, was obvious and very gratifying
to see.

In addition to the information I shared with you in our meeting, I thought
of another project I worked on that reflects the kind of contribution I could
make as a member of Miller's product development team. The details of
that project (the proposal and the final report, both of which I authored) are
enclosed for your review.

As soon as you're through interviewing the other candidates, I'd appreciate
hearing from you, and would be pleased meet with you again. I can be
reached at home in the evening as well as at my office during the day.

Sincerely yours,

Geraldine McMahon
(987) 654-3210 (h)
(987) 543-2106 (w)

SAMPLE RESIGNATION LETTER- FORMAL

Your Name
Your Address
Your City, State, Zip Code
Your Phone Number
Your Email

Date

Name
Title
Organization
Address
City, State, Zip Code

Dear Mr./Ms. Last Name:

Please accept this letter as formal notification that I intend to leave my position with XYZ Company on September 15.

Thank you for the opportunities you have provided me during my time with the company.

If I can be of any assistance during this transition, please let me know.

Sincerely,

Your Signature

SAMPLE RESIGNATION LETTER

August 15, 2012

Mr. Jim Hughes
Smith Consulting
New York, NY 01001

Dear Jim,

I am writing to confirm that I am resigning from my position as Assistant Actuary at Smith Consulting on September 1, 2012.

Although there is no written contract of employment between us, I understand that we have a verbal agreement and that my notice period stands at two weeks. Please be assured that I will do all that I can to assist you in a smooth transfer of my responsibilities before leaving.

I wish both you and Smith Consulting every good fortune and I would like to thank you for having me as part of your actuarial team.

Sincerely,

Margaret Jones

SAMPLE RESIGNATION LETTER

December 10, 2012

Ms Mary McCarthy
XYZ Insurance Company
55 Madison Ave
New York, NY 20439

Dear Mary,

I am submitting my written notice of resignation from XYZ Insurance Company effective two weeks from today. My last day will be December 24, 2012.

I will be happy to help train my replacement and/or anything else you feel will help make the transition smoother.

Thank you so much, Mary. My experience at XYZ Insurance has been rewarding and productive, and I wish only the best for you and for the company.

Sincerely,

Susan Sullivan

Dan Pederson

1600 Main Street, Ann Arbor, MI 55555
555-555-5555
dpederson25@gmail.com

Disciplined professional experienced in financial markets with excellent interpersonal skills seeks career as an actuarial analyst

EXAMS

- SOA Exam P: May, 2013

EDUCATION

University of Michigan   Ann Arbor, MI   5/2013
- M.S.E. FINANCIAL ENGINEERING
- GPA: 3.59/4.00
- Emphasis on statistical analysis, structuring and pricing derivative securities, interest rate modelling, Monte Carlo simulation, VaR
- Computer Skills: Excel, SPSS, C++, Matlab, Mathematica

University of Michigan,   Ann Arbor, MI   5/2011
- B.A. Mathematics
- GPA: 3.64/4.00 (with Honors)

EXPERIENCE

Assent Trading, LLC   Chicago, IL   6/2013-present
Futures Trader
- Trade CBOT Mini-Dow, Big Dow and CME E-mini Russell 2000 financial futures contracts electronically.
- Develop and program proprietary trading strategies implemented through trading interface API.
- Use Matlab and MS Excel for statistical analysis of trades and risk management

Outward Bound Mexico, seasonal employment during summers of 2010, 2011, 2012
Instructor
- Taught leadership, teamwork and communications skills to participants through outdoor activities such as jungle trekking, rock climbing, sailing and kayaking

University of Michigan,   Ann Arbor, Michigan   (9/2010-6/2011)
Research Assistant
- Worked with doctoral students on research projects in biochemical engineering

ADDITIONAL
Pi Mu Epsilon, National Mathematics Honor Society
Tau Beta Pi, National Engineering Honor Society
AASI-Certified Snowboard Instructor
University of Michigan Rugby Club
Fluent in Spanish

SAMPLE RÉSUMÉ 2: Actuarial student working at a life and annuity carrier

Nancy Sullivan

5 Elm St. Ardmore, PA Cell: (555) 666-7777
Email: nsullivanactuary@gmail.com

WORK EXPERIENCE

Large Global Insurer, Philadelphia, PA

Group Benefits Division: Life & Accident Pricing—
Sr. Actuarial Analyst   5/2013-Present

- Actuarial resource for various projects designed to increase the company's voluntary benefits market share

Fixed Deferred Annuity Pricing & Product Management—
Sr. Actuarial Analyst   8/2012-5/2013

- Responsible for the bi-weekly Deferred Fixed Annuity rate setting process for new business and renewals
- Investigated creative solutions to reduce risk and increase profitability of the Fixed Deferred Annuity block of business

Group Benefits Division: Life & Accident Pricing—
Sr. Actuarial Analyst   6/2011-8/2012

- Utilized Predictive Modeling to enhance the Group Life manual rating algorithm; Ensured pricing adequacy of a $1B block of business by leveraging modeling results, close ratios, and competitor information; coordinated implementation with Underwriting and Sales; communicated results to senior leadership
- Consulted with Underwriting and Sales on an ongoing basis to accurately price cases while balancing top and bottom lines
- Presented to senior Actuarial leadership on the various new and innovative means
- Trained three new members of the team, including manager
- Increased pricing accuracy and overall efficiency of the Life Retiree Buyout model using basic and advanced VBA

Leadership, Communication, and Innovation

- Worked on a cross-functional project team to create and execute a digital commerce marketing plan to drive additional new business growth and support existing programs in the Association space
- Actively participate in on-campus recruiting, as well as both the intern and full-time mentor programs

Large Domestic Insurer, Philadelphia, PA

Large Group Commercial Insurance—Actuarial Intern   May-August 2010

- Completed a thorough audit of the department's rating engine and worked on the manual rating analysis for several states

RELEVANT SKILLS

Microsoft Office (Excel, PowerPoint, Access, Word, Outlook), VBA, SAP Business Objects

EDUCATION

Pennsylvania State University, State College, PA
Bachelor of Science in Actuarial Science, May 2011
Passed SOA Exam P/1 and SOA Exam FM/2
Graduated Summa Cum Laude

HONORS AND ACTIVITIES

Actuarial Science Club	*President*	Fall 2009-Spring 2011
Actuarial Science Club	*Member*	Fall 2007-Spring 2009
Full Tuition Presidential Scholarship	*Recipient*	Fall 2007-Spring 2011

SAMPLE RÉSUMÉ 3: Actuarial student working for a health insurer

Mary Olson
19 Monroe Avenue
Scarsdale, NY 20202
Mary.olson@gmail.com

EXPERIENCE

Major Health Insurer, New York, NY.

Actuarial Analyst   *January 2002-present*

- Responsible for calculating savings based on Cost of Care initiatives
- Responsible for updating Admin, Profit and Commission tables for Integrated Rating Project
- Prepare monthly reserves for commercial business
- Produce monthly Cost of Care reports
- Developed a Broker Compensation model
- Involved in developing rates for small groups including pricing for non-standard benefits
- Supported Vendor Teams
- Evaluated risk-sharing arrangements for Medicare Risk Products
- Developed a Performance Based Model to calculate settlements with providers
- Designed and implemented a new methodology to calculate reserves for Medicare Risk

Major Health Insurer, Chicago, IL.

Individual Health Actuarial Intern   *Summer 2000*

- Designed SAS programs to perform various data queries.
- Produced analyses of claims experience and competitors' rates.
- Prepared rate increase filings in various states.

Merrill Lynch, Boston, MA. *Financial Advisor Assistant*   *Spring 2000*

- Developed an investment strategy based on a 4-month study of a stock basket's performance.
- Maintained and updated existing client portfolios.
- Assisted financial advisor's marketing efforts to obtain new clients.

EXAMS

Society of Actuaries/Casualty Actuarial Society Exams: Passed Courses 1-4

EDUCATION

Boston College, Chestnut Hill, MA
Graduated Magna Cum Laude, May 2001, double major in Finance and Mathematics

COMPUTER SKILLS

MS Word, Excel, Power Point. Programming in FORTRAN, C++, and SAS

Jacob Levine

215 East 86th Street, New York, NY 10021 jacob.b.levine@yahoo.com

Large Casualty Insurer, New York, NY (February 2011-present)
Assistant Actuary, Corporate Actuarial and Risk Management

Corporate Reserving. Contribute to creating and documenting controls to ensure compliance with Sarbanes-Oxley in corporate reserving practices. Develop a construction defect methodology which was subsequently adopted by actuaries at the enterprise level. Analyze and model both direct and assumed asbestos and environmental reserves.

Dynamic Financial Analysis (DFA). Manage the building of stochastic parameterization of pricing, reserving, credit, and asset risks in a robust model of P&C business. Applications of the project included:

Reinsurance Analysis—Successfully recommend raising of per-risk retentions.

Capital Allocation - Create an allocation framework to facilitate calculation of risk-adjusted return on capital.

Rating Agency Negotiation—Support company's negotiations with rating agencies for insurance strength ratings, including modeling of probability of ruin and capital adequacy testing.

Stochastic Reserving. Manage a comprehensive stochastic review of diverse reserving lines. Aggregated marginal reserve distributions within a correlation structure via copula assumption. Present results and analysis to executive leadership with positive outcome on reserving practice and philosophy. Recommend overall reserve level and demonstrate the necessary adjustments to balance reserve risk among individual lines.

Large Insurance Company, Los Angeles, CA (October 2008-January 2011)
Actuarial Analyst III, Workers Compensation Pricing

Performed actuarial analysis for rate change filings. Created and maintained interactive intranet-based financial reports monitoring underwriting results, discretionary pricing, and exposure distributions. Calculated residual market burdens. Significant special projects included aggregate loss distribution modeling, research on state guarantee funds, analysis of claim adjusters' utilization of MIRA, a case reserving tool based on multivariate regression, and development of a novel and unique algorithm to analytically calculate on level earned premium.

Big 4 Consulting Firm, New York, NY (August 2005-September 2008)

Actuarial Associate

Programmed and executed valuations of defined-benefit pension plans for IRS funding and FASB accounting purposes. Produced year-end financial disclosure information for clients' retirement liabilities, assets, and periodic pension costs.

Designations

CASUALTY ACTUARIAL SOCIETY MEMBERSHIP: Associate 2009

Education

Large State University, *Bachelor of Science in Statistics, Emphasis in Actuarial Science,* 2005. Course work included econometrics, inferential statistics, operations research, actuarial models, numerical analysis, SAS programming. Attended on full academic scholarship.

Alison M. Smith

125 Ashbrook Drive, Naperville, IL, 20202 alismith3489@yahoo.com

WORK EXPERIENCE

Feb 2008 - Present   **Large Leading Consulting Firm, Chicago, IL**
September 2011-Present   *Consulting Actuary*

- Worked directly with 5 senior salespeople and management of the U.S. and U.K. offices for the firms marketing initiative of the Bermudian market. Participated in the Capital Committee of the industry body, Bermuda International Long-Term Insurers and Reinsurers (BILTIR), regarding the recent regulation change in Bermuda.
- Assisted a small-sized insurer in assessing capital requirements under various regimes. Bermuda Solvency Capital Requirements (BSCR), S&P, NAIC RBC, and Solvency II were covered.
- Assisted a listed U.S. insurer in assessing the economic value (embedded value) of their fixed annuity block as part of the holistic strategy to tackle challenges from the low interest rate environment.
- Led a team of 5 on a time-sensitive project validating a financial projection model of Variable Universal Life (VUL). Adopted a more effective approach. Tight deadline was met and the modified model passed all requirements required by the firm's VUL subject expert.
- Worked directly with the lead of the firm's ERM thought leadership team to help position the firm in the U.S. marketplace. Directly communicated and addressed inquiries from U.S. senior salespersons regarding all ERM issues.

February 2008-September 2011   London, United Kingdom

- Engaged in numerous projects in Europe. Half of the tenure spent at client sites with clients' local representatives.
- Led a team of 5 and reported directly to client's Chief Actuary in advising a leading insurer on product and capital strategy, taking conflicting interests among stakeholders including regulators, shareholders, and policyholders into consideration. Proposed a strategic asset allocation solution, lowering risk borne by the insurer while maintaining the dividend they delivered to their policyholders. Assured the regulator that solvency and policyholders' interests were well protected.

- Seconded to a leading UK insurer for 10 months for the domestication of their Hong Kong business. The secondment included a risk alignment exercise on an economic capital basis and analysis of advanced management rules in response to different economic environments and dynamic policyholder behaviours. Key responsibilities included high-level result review and communicating results to the Chief Actuary and the head office.
- Assisted a leading insurer in assessing the opportunity of Universal Life in the mass and mass affluent markets. Project scope included identification of financial risks from each product design and assessment of causes, drivers, and risk management of each identified financial risk.
- Advised a small-sized insurer and consulted directly to the C-suite executives for a potential strategic partnership to expand market share. Interviewed heads of each department to understand their operations and strengths. Identified client's bargaining chips in negotiating partnerships with big players and proposed alternatives to gain market share.

EDUCATION AND PROFESSIONAL QUALIFICATIONS

March 2012,   **Fellow of the Society of Actuaries (FSA)**

February, 2011 **Chartered Enterprise Risk Analyst (CERA)**

December 2007, **Drake University, Bachelor of Science, Actuarial Science**

Kimberly A. Smith

4728 E. Palm Lane
Phoenix, AZ 85008
(280) 540-4444

Work Experience

March 1999-Present
Senior Actuarial Assistant, ABC Consulting, Phoenix, AZ

Responsibilities:

- Annual pension plan valuations for several clients with various plan features and funding methods. Handle data issues, calculate liabilities both in actuarial software and spreadsheets, analyze gain/loss scenarios, prepare final actuarial reports including plan funded status, amortization bases for plan amendments or changes in assumptions, minimum and maximum contribution amounts
- Actuarial equivalence and benefit calculations for defined benefit pensions requiring interpretation of plan documents and compliance with IRS and PBGC regulations and guidelines
- Retiree medical plan valuations and SFAS 106 disclosure
- FAS 87/132 reporting, including pension expense
- Annual benefit statements for active pension plan participants
- Routine regulatory filings including IRS Form 5500 with attachments and PBGC Form 1 including Schedule A

Major Projects:

- Created VBA program to integrate multiple sourced data into standard fields and prepare for valuation system input
- Modeled changes to a defined contribution pension plan in a VBA benefit illustrator that was distributed as an Excel file to plan participants. This application served as a model for two subsequent illustrators.
- Converted two pension plan valuation programs into new internal software
- Integrated new defined benefit pension client into our systems and procedures. Determined prior actuary's assumptions and methodology, created benefit calculation spreadsheet, set up liability program

- With input from senior consultants, developed defined benefit pension plan administrative forms for client use to comply with regulatory requirements and streamline administration process. These forms are now templates.
- Reviewed benefit calculations and administrative procedures for a large defined benefit plan compliance review
- Obtained and compiled retirement benefit survey results from various California city and county pension plans to assist a client county with union negotiations
- Researched and analyzed different asset valuation methods to minimize the cost of clients' poor asset returns

Actuarial Exams:
- Exam 160, Survival Models, May 1999
- Exam 120, Statistical Methods, November 1999

May 1997-March 1999
Actuarial Assistant, Large Insurer, Los Angeles, California

Responsibilities:
- Monthly GAAP, statutory and tax financial reporting for the entity, including preparation of statements, reserve analysis using rollforward reports, and calculation of reserves produced outside the main system
- Preparation and analysis of monthly lapse reports
- Quarterly surrenderability analysis for the Actuarial Financial Package that is utilized by senior management to maintain adequate reserve levels and identify trends in the various product lines
- Annual Statement and state filing preparation
- Fiscal year end tax reserve reporting
- Valuation of annuities for policyowner service and claims departments
- Sample valuation calculations and explanations at the request of financial auditors and state examiners
- Documentation of procedures and routine reserve calculation and verification

Major Projects:
- Created MS Access database to automate year end financial reporting and industry rating agency surveys by downloading data from the mainframe using SAS and constructing queries
- Prepared liability modeling for cash flow testing of deferred and immediate annuities using PTS

- Modeled IndexAmerica to comply with current NAIC equity index valuation guidelines with the assistance of Karin Doerr
- Provided detailed sample calculations of excess interest adjustments to assist MIS in programming of reserves for the Sterling Select fixed annuity products
- Evaluated reinsurance business to determine product types and valuation standards for proper liability modeling and financial reporting

Actuarial Exams:

- Exam 150, Actuarial Mathematics, May 1998
- Exam 151, Risk Theory, November 1997

April 1994--October 1996
Actuarial Assistant, Large Insurance Group, Philadelphia, PA

Responsibilities:

- Managed computer calculations of reserves and inforce exhibits for quarterly financial reporting
- Prepared liability portions of the Annual Statement by constructing specific queries on the AS/400
- Calculated reserves in spreadsheets for supplementary contracts; WP and disability income, disabled and active lives; deficiency reserves; reserves for cash values in excess of reserves
- Calculated cash values for various types of life insurance including double protection to age 65, retirement income at 70, and 15 year decreasing term
- Provided and explained information to financial auditors and insurance examiners
- Administered ceded reinsurance business by overseeing submission process, submitting claims, reconciling monthly billing statements and assisting in recaptures

Major Projects:

- Supported the reprogramming of entire valuation system. Contributions included determining and verifying reserve calculations for all Exhibit 8 numbers.
- Worked closely with Data Processing Department to automate daily tasks such as cash value and universal life account value calculations, and the development of summary reports necessary for statements.
- Assisted company actuary in generating a cash flow testing system

Actuarial Exams:

- ◆ Exam 100, Calculus and Linear Algebra, November 1994
- ◆ Exam 110, Probability and Statistics, November 1995
- ◆ Exam 130, Operations Research, November 1995
- ◆ Exam 140, Theory of Interest, May 1996

August 1993--May 1994

Graduate Assistant, Arizona State University, Mathematics Department, Tempe, AZ

Responsibilities:

- ◆ Worked minimum of five hours per week in tutoring center, tutoring all lower division math subjects
- ◆ Created and edited test questions
- ◆ Scored exams

GRE:

- ◆ Analytical 800 (99th percentile)
- ◆ Quantitative 740 (87th percentile)
- ◆ Verbal 700 (94th percentile)

Education

August 1993--May 1994

Arizona State University, Tempe, Arizona, Master of Science in Statistical Science with Industrial Engineering as a related field. Only completed 6 credit hours due to health reasons.

August 1989--December 1992

Arizona State University, Tempe, Arizona, Bachelor of Science in General Mathematics. Graduated Cum Laude with 3.5 cumulative GPA, 3.8 graduating semester.

August 1988--May 1989

University of Arizona, Tucson, Arizona, Education Major. Completed general education courses.

SAMPLE RÉSUMÉ 7: Experienced FSA, working in insurance

Linda Yang
864 Fourth Avenue, Seattle, WA 33467
lyang_Seattle@gmail.com

Experience LARGE MULTILINE INSURER, Seattle, WA **April 2001-Current**
Actuary—Managing Actuary—AVP—Vice President & Actuary

- Develop, price, implement, and quarterly-value fixed, variable, and modified separate account life products using statutory, IFRS/GAAP, and market-consistent (Solv II) frameworks.
- Set and manage non-guaranteed elements rates for UL, MSA, and ISWL COLI blocks.
- Manage and train student- through Fellow-level actuaries, underwriter/support staff, forms/compliance managers, and contractors. Serve as resource for senior leaders and members of marketing, legal, operations, systems, fund management, and investment teams.
- Reinsurance Manager: Negotiate, draft, execute, and recapture YRT, coins, funds-withheld coins, modco, and stop-loss treaties for domestic, international, and transnational deals. Assist risk, admin, and accounting staff with treaty implementation and review/approve monthly processing.
- Policy form filing, drafting, reasonableness tests, and certifications on a $10 billion mixed UL, VUL (registered & private placement), and MSA block. IIPRC and extensive SEC experience.
- Life underwriter for guarantee-issue B/COLI groups.
- Created dynamic risk transfer program for experience-rated groups, evaluation/elevation process for institutional case restructures, and quarterly performance metrics summary.
- Stable value investment products—negotiation, contract drafting, pricing, and implementation.

LARGE GLOBAL INSURER, Chicago, IL

January 1997-April 2001

Assistant Actuary—Actuary—Vice President & Actuary

- Designed and priced individual and second-to-die VUL, UL, ULSG, and ISWL for wholesaler, independent broker, employee-agent, and bank channels.
- Managed implementation and reinsurance of VUL, UL, ULSG, VA, EIA, and MVAA products.
- Actuarial support for SEC and state product filings, marketing materials, and sales/marketing.
- *Ad hoc* M&A modeling; product support staff trainer, managed student and credentialed actuaries.

MEDIUM SIZED INSURER—Indianapolis, IN

May 1991-January 1997

Actuarial Rotations: Product development, group major medical benefits, reinsurance, and valuation.

Education   **1997,** Fellow of the Society of Actuaries
1991, BA in Mathematics/Actuarial Science, Purdue University

Additional   Company Leadership Academy and Executive Presentations graduate.

SAMPLE RÉSUMÉ 8: Experienced FCAS

THOMAS SAMPLE
110 Stacy Drive
Fords, NJ 08863
Work: (973) 222 - 1111

EXPERIENCE

SAMPLE RE, Midtown, NJ, 1998 - Present
Chief Actuary of the Runoff Operation (Nov. 1, 2002-Present)
Responsible for $3.8 billion loss reserves
Certify loss reserves and loss expense reserves for subsidiary companies

Assistant Vice President (Prior to 11/1/2002)

- Assist in annual strategic planning regarding premium volume, loss ratios, combined ratios to achieve the desired GAAP results for upcoming years.
- Establish IBNR reserve as well as premium accruals for all lines of business, both traditional as well as finite reinsurance.
- Translate underwriting year actuarial loss and premium indications into calendar year / quarter financial impacts; communicate the results and explain the main drivers to the responsible underwriting department and senior management.
- Interact with Pricing Unit and review pricing models to evaluate the assumptions used in reserve analysis.
- Interact with external auditors and provide explanations and supporting work papers for actuarial related inquires.
- Work on Ad hoc projects such as calculation of accident year loss experience based on underwriting year indications, letter of credits and cash flow analysis

PINNACLE REINSURANCE COMPANY, New York, NY, 1997-1998
Associate Actuary and Assistant Secretary

- Performed quarterly and year-end loss and LAE reserve analysis for all lines of business.
- Prepared actuarial reports to fulfill various external reporting requirements.
- Performed contract commutation analysis.

- Coordinated with IT Department to obtain workable and useful data information.
- Provided actuarial service for claim servicing company.

STATE **I**NSURANCE **D**EPARTMENT, City, State, 1989-1997
Supervising Actuary
- Performed independent reserve analysis for companies under State examination.
- Meeting with company representatives to present and discuss reserve findings.
- Evaluated reinsurance contracts for risk transfer analysis.
- Supervised student actuaries in gathering, preparing and reconciling loss data and exhibits.
- Worked on Industry Special Projects:
    - <u>Catastrophe Reserves</u>: compiled industry data and calculated relative catastrophe exposure factors by state; researched/incorporated appropriate inflation and population indices for trending; participated in meetings and conference calls with working group members for further enhancement.
    - <u>Risk Based Capital (RBC)</u>: coordinated with NAIC in calculating reserve and premium RBC factors and investment income factors; documented procedures and instructions;
    - Performed sensitivity test using sample companies' data, demonstrated sample calculations for the Department employees.
- Reviewed Statement of Actuarial Opinions to identify qualified or deficient opinions.
- Participated in current event committee meetings.

PROFESSIONAL   Fellow of the Casualty Actuarial Society (FCAS), November 2002

Member of the American Academy of Actuaries (MAAA), November 1996

COMPUTER   Lotus, Excel, Access, Word

EDUCATION   BA Computer Science / Mathematics, 1989: <u>Medium Sized University, New York, NY</u>